WILDLIFE
The Beauty of Animals

THE IMAGE BANK®

ISBN 0-941267-17-2

Manufactured in Spain

Producer : Ted Smart
Author : Rupert O Matthews
Book Design : Sara Cooper
Photo Research : Annie Price
Production Assistant : Seni Glaister

**All photographs in this book
appear courtesy of Survival Anglia Ltd
with the exception of,**

Page 2/3 Natural Science Photos
Page 108/109 Wayne Lankinen
Page 114/115 Tom and Pat Leeson
Page 134/135 Eric Meola, The Image Bank
Page 138 G + J Images/K Will, The Image Bank
Page 144/145 Lex Hes, Natural Science Photos

There are over one million different types of animal on Earth today. Each kind of animal has unique features. The types look different from each other, find their food in different ways and are quite distinct from other species. There are however, certain features which group animals together into genus, family or class. Scientists make use of such features to categorise animals into 'cats', 'dogs' or 'lizards'. Each animal in the group shares characteristics with the other which are not found in animals of other groups.

The most basic grouping is between animals with a backbone and those without. The invertebrates, which lack a backbone, are by far the most numerous both in absolute numbers and in the variety of species. Some species lack a skeleton at all, such as the jellyfish and amoebas, but most have a skeletal system which encloses the body. These are the crabs, crustaceans and insects.

Of these the most numerous are the insects, and in fact the insects can be said to be the most successful group of creatures the world has ever known. They first evolved many hundreds of millions of years ago, before the first dinosaurs stalked the Earth, and have flourished ever since. There are thought to be about one million species of insects, though nobody is entirely certain how many there really are. It has been said that any naturalist wanting to discover a new species need only walk through the Congo rain forest armed with a butterfly net for an hour or two to be certain of catching at least one previously undescribed type of insect. At the same time the destruction of large areas of wilderness means that several species are exterminated each year, often without anyone being aware that they existed.

The incredible variety of insect life is, in part, due to the extraordinary degree of specialisation which the different species can show. The yucca moth (*Tegeticula alba*), for example is adapted to co-exist with the yucca plant. When ready to lay its eggs the female moth visits a yucca flower and collects a quantity of pollen. It then flies to a different yucca and deposits the pollen on the stigma, thus fertilising the seeds. The moth then lays its eggs in the flower and departs. The eggs are timed to hatch at the moment when the seeds have developed enough to provide food for the caterpillars. The moth larvae therefore have a ready-made source of nourishment on which they thrive before pupating into adults. The yucca also benefits for some seeds are usually left to develop into seedlings.

Such diversity and adaptability is made possible by the tough exoskeleton which the insects have developed. Completely encasing the insect's body is a layer of strong chiton. This acts not only as armour, but also as an anchorage for the muscles, giving shape to the whole animal. As such the exoskeleton is remarkably successful and insects can withstand pressures, relative to their body size, far greater than any other animal. But it has its drawbacks, one of which is that the animal cannot grow and expand because it is encased in a solid shell of armour. Insects get around this problem by periodically moulting their skin. The old, rigid skin is split open and the insect, surrounded by a soft new skin emerges. Puffing its body up, the insect pushes its new skin into a larger shape before it dries and hardens into a rigid shell. At such a time the insect is almost shapeless and powerless to move. This makes it vulnerable to attack, and many fall victim to predators.

The higher animals lack the exoskeleton and instead have an internal skeleton. These are the vertebrates, animals with backbones. The earliest vertebrates were fish, which first appeared over 500 million years ago and are still the most numerous. Vertebrates have the enormous advantage that their skeleton can grow with them, so they never need undergo the vulnerable stage of skin-shedding. When vertebrates moved on to the land in the form of amphibians some 390 million years ago they were faced with the problem of supporting their bodies. Denied the support of water, the land-based amphibians had to keep themselves upright and be able to move around. They solved both problems by converting their fins into legs.

Amphibians were the most advanced animals on earth for millions of years, but have now been overtaken by several other groups. They do however remain an important part of the fauna in many areas. Amphibians are, by definition, tied to the water both during their everyday lives and for reproduction. Indeed some species are never found more than a few feet from ponds or streams.

The skins of the vast majority of amphibians are moist and covered with mucus. Many absorb oxygen through their skins in addition to their lungs. It is therefore essential that they keep their skins damp. Amphibians must also return to ponds or streams to breed for their eggs are soft and soon shrivel and die if exposed to air.

Most amphibians live within reach of permanent ponds and streams so that when the breeding season arrives they can make their way to these hatcheries. In many cases the ponds take on the role of ancestral homes where generation after generation of amphibian has been hatched, grown and in time laid eggs.

There are some species, however, which live far from permanent water. Some toads burrow beneath arid plains or forests where there is little in the way of running water. Instead these creatures rely on the ephemeral bodies of water which appear after the infrequent rains. As soon as the patter of rain drops and the rising level of humidity alerts the toads to the presence of water they dig their way to the surface and hurry downhill in the hope of finding a wet hollow. Leaping into the water, the toads sing so as to attract other toads, mate and then hurry back to their burrows. The eggs hatch quickly and the young develop rapidly so as to become adults before the temporary pools dry out.

A few species of frog find their homes in even more unlikely places, in the branches of trees. These tree frogs, which are generally found in tropical areas, are specially adapted to their arboreal homes. They have extremely powerful legs, able to propel them from one branch to another, and keen eyesight to guide their spectacular leaps. The feet of tree frogs are splayed and each toe equipped with special gripping pads to enable the frogs to hold on to twigs and branches. This is necessary as a single slip might result in a fall from a height of fifty feet which would be catastrophic. So firm is the grip of the tree frog that it can climb vertical sheets of glass with ease.

Breeding presents tree frogs with something of a problem. If they were to breed in pools or streams they would need to leave the cover of foliage and expose themselves to attack on the ground. They have, got round the problem by relying on the tiny pockets of water which collect in holes in trees and in the junctions of branches. Such pools are necessarily small and often short-lived. Because of this many species have learnt to care for their eggs, by moving them to new pools if the original threatens to dry out.

The vast majority of amphibians are carnivorous. The smaller species preying on invertebrates, such as insects and earthworms, and the larger taking small reptiles and mammals. Amphibians cannot properly chew their food, nor bite off chunks of flesh. They must therefore swallow their prey whole, cramming them into their gaping mouths with their forelegs. The small teeth are used simply to hold victims, while some amphibians do not have any teeth at all.

Reptiles are quite different for they have a very varied diet. Tortoises eat plants, biting through great quantities of food with their horny beaks, while the marine iguana dives into the Pacific to feed on seaweed. Chameleons concentrate on eating insects, as are several lizards. Snakes, a highly specialised group of reptiles, may take lizards, eggs, rodents and even young cattle, depending on their size.

But it is not the more widespread diet which distinguishes reptiles from amphibians. It is the fact that they have freed themselves from a total dependence on water. The reptiles have achieved this in two ways. First by insulating their own bodies from the drying effects of the air and second by removing their reproductive cycle from the water.

The first is achieved by having a scaly skin, a feature shared by all reptiles. This impervious skin is made up of a collection of horny scales which is dry and completely impervious to water. This protects the internal fluids of the reptile's body from evaporation and removes the need for frequent dips in water. In most reptiles the scaly skin is made up of a layer of small horny scales forming a continuous barrier just below the epidermis, or outer layer of skin. This structure allows for only limited growth within the same skin and such animals need to moult periodically.

Some reptiles, notably crocodiles, have bony nodules in their skin around which the scales of horn grow. Because these scales increase in size each year, the animal does not need to shed its skin. Instead there is a gradual increase in skin surface to match the increasing body size of the animal. Indeed the fact that such animals continue to grow each year has led to speculation that they can reach truly enormous sizes. It is known that lengths of 20 feet are not at all unusual for the estuarine crocodiles (*Crocodylus prorsus*) of Australia and southeast Asia. In the 1950s a particularly large specimen, measuring over 28 feet was shot, and travellers' tales talk of animals larger still. It is known that the long extinct *Deinosuchus* reached a length of over 52 feet, so perhaps such stories contain some truth.

In tortoises and turtles, the development of bony plates has been taken to is ultimate extreme. The bony cores are distributed across the upper and lower parts of the body, while the horny sheaths grow out to meet each other in a solid shell. As the tortoise grows, the horny sheaths form a new lower layer which is slightly larger than the one above. Since such new layers form each year the shell, or carapace, gradually increases in thickness as time passes. The

annual growth rings also allow the age of a tortoise to be judged fairly accurately, at least for the first years of its life. Old tortoises, however, tend to lose the topmost, and oldest, layers of each plate and so have fewer annual rings than they merit.

The largest, and longest lived of all tortoises are the giant tortoises which live on various islands throughout the world. These huge animals, over five feet in length and 600 pounds in weight, can live for over 130 years. They are mostly found on the Seychelles, where over 100,000 thrive on the islands, isolated from predators. The Galapagos giant tortoise is much rarer, indeed it is extinct on some of the islands, and is strictly protected.

In the past, however, the tortoises enjoyed no such status and their story echoes the fate of many interesting island species. Because of the isolated nature of island habitats, certain groups of creatures are often absent. This was true of the Seychelles and Galapagos islands where both competitors for food and also predators were absent. The tortoises were therefore able to increase in size and lost their fear of attack.

When European sailors first reached these islands in the 18th century, the very factors which had previously helped the tortoises, now proved to be both disastrous and of benefit. The sailors, accustomed to dried meat and biscuits, found fresh tortoise meat irresistible and slaughtered large numbers of them. The fact that there were no natural predators on the islands meant that the tortoises were unafraid of man and, almost literally, walked into the cooking pot. On some islands overhunting led to the total extinction.

In other instances the sailors, realising the benefits of a ready food supply, captured tortoises alive and carried them to other islands. There the creatures were set loose and established breeding populations. After two centuries of extinction and artificial distribution it is now impossible to be certain which islands originally supported populations of giant tortoises and which did not.

If the skin of reptiles has proved to be a boon, both by reason of its impervious and its protective nature, the reptile egg is even more important. Amphibian eggs are soft and permeable to water. If they were laid on dry ground they would distort and rapidly dry out, thus killing the embryonic creature within. Reptile eggs can safely be laid in the driest conditions, indeed it is essential that they be kept out of the water.

The internal structures of the reptile eggs are basically very similar to those of the amphibian. Both contain an embryonic creature together with reserves of food, but there the similarities end. The reptilian egg is surrounded by a tough shell which protects the embryo from attack and, more crucially, prevents dessication. Thus the reptile can lay its egg on dry land.

The shell itself, however, causes problems. Not only does it prevent dessication, it also slows down the vital absorption of oxygen from the surrounding air and the expellation of carbon dioxide. The egg has therefore developed a circulatory system of its own, with vessels carrying blood from the embryo to the shell and back again, exchanging the gasses. At the same time the growing creature is absorbing food from the yolk and producing waste product. In an amphibian egg such materials pass directly out into the surrounding water, but they cannot pass through the shell of a reptile's egg. Nor can they remain in contact with the embryo for they are often poisonous. A special sac called the allantois has developed to absorb the waste products and to isolate them from the growing embryo.

As the embryo gradually develops into a young reptile it is provided with everything it needs. It has water and food already in the egg, while oxygen can be absorbed from the surrounding air and waste products isolated in the allantois. By the time the young reptile hatches out it is perfectly formed and able to fend for itself in the world at large.

Armed with the revolutionary egg and a scaly skin the reptiles first evolved about 300 million years ago. They spread and evolved rapidly so that by around 270 million years ago they were the dominant form of life on land. With their improved breeding mechanism they pushed the more vulnerable amphibians from many habitats, and moved into dry areas where amphibians had never reached, even establishing themselves in deserts.

Over the following 60 million years the reptiles continued to evolve and to diversify and so produced a large number of different groups. Among these were groups still to be found today, including the tortoises, lizards and rhynchocephalians. But far more important at the time was a group now referred to as archosaurs, which translates as 'the ruling reptiles'. Initially the archosaurs were a fairly small group of semi-aquatic reptiles which seem to have been predominantly hunters of other reptiles and the amphibians.

They splashed through swamps, running on four legs or using their strong tails to power them through deeper water. Before long the archosaurs themselves divided into a number of different groups. One, the crocodilians, retained the lifestyle of the earlier archosaurs. Indeed they have changed remarkably little down to the present day and remain powerful hunters which lurk in shallow water and in swamps.

Two further groups which emerged from the archosaurs, the ornithischians and saurischians, developed extremely similar adaptations for a life on dry land. Though the actual relationship between the two groups remains unclear, they are commonly referred to together as the dinosaurs. Both groups of dinosaurs altered their bodies to achieve what is known as the fully erect posture. This means that the legs are tucked beneath the body, a feature which confers many benefits. In most reptiles, including lizards and tortoises, the legs splay outwards. This involves considerable physical effort to lift the body when moving. With legs standing vertically down from the body, however, the weight rests on the bones, and muscles are brought into play only for movement.

Dinosaurs took advantage of this, and other physical improvements, to dominate other forms of terrestrial life throughout the world. The earliest dinosaurs were rather small, many of them two-legged carnivores. But as time passed they diversified and multiplied to produce a wide range of species each suited to a particular role. The dinosaurs built up a total ecology with plant-eaters, hunters, scavengers and omnivores, together with a few creatures whose lifestyle remains unclear.

Perhaps the largest dinosaur of all was the beast known as *Ultrasaurus*, a huge herbivore which measured over 100 feet in length and may have weighed about 140 tons, as much as the largest whale alive today. If these estimates prove to be true, the *Ultrasaurus* would have been the largest animal ever to have lived. Beside such giants even the largest meat-eaters would have appeared small. The mighty *Tyrannosaurus* was around 40 feet long and was equipped with massive talons and teeth over 7 inches in length with which to deal out death to its prey. Beside these giants lived smaller plant-eaters analogous to modern gazelles and tiny predators which led lives similar to modern foxes and wildcats.

A further group of archosaur descendants took to a life which could not be further removed from that of the crocodiles and dinosaurs, though they flourished at the same time as the latter. Pterosaurs became much lighter, lost their heavy limbs and developed enormously long fore limbs which supported a flap of leathery skin. These fore limbs became wings on which the pterosaurs could fly and soar high above the ancient world. It is unfortunate that no fossils have survived which reveal exactly how the aquatic archosaurs evolved into airborne pterosaurs.

Even more remarkable was the fact that the pterosaurs evolved a completely different metabolism from all other reptiles. Instead of relying on the heat of the surrounding environment to warm their bodies, pterosaurs were able to generate their heat internally by chemical means. Such a step was vital for the pterosaurs. By producing internal heat the animals were able to keep their bodily functions moving at a steady rate, no matter what the temperature of the surrounding air. For a flying animal this is essential, otherwise a blast of cold air would cut the power the flight muscles could develop and plunge the creature into a fatal dive.

From about 200 million years ago for about 140 million years the more advanced archosaur descendants, the pterosaurs and dinosaurs, were the dominant forms of life on Earth. They filled every available ecological niche on land and in the air. Then, suddenly, they were gone. Nobody is entirely certain what caused the sudden demise of the dinosaurs and pterosaurs. Some scientists look for the explanation in climatic changes or in the operation of the food chains. Others seek more dramatic answers and postulate that a collision between the Earth and a massive comet may have sealed the fate of these highly successful creatures. The truth is simply, that nobody can be certain.

Whatever happened the close of the geological period known as the Cretaceous, some 64 million years ago, marked the end of the reptile dominance of the world. The largest and most important groups, such as the dinosaurs and pterosaurs, died out completely. Not a single species survived. Even among those creatures which did survive, the number of species declined catastrophically. Among the Rhynchocephalians, once a very numerous group, only one species now exists, and that only on isolated islets off New Zealand.

Among the reptilian groups to continue relatively unscathed by the mass extinctions were the lizards, or squamata. These small animals continue to thrive in large numbers. They are particularly common in warm climates where they can soak up enough heat to keep their bodies functioning at high metabolic rates, enabling them to compete with the mammals and other advanced animals on an equal footing. Tortoises and turtles likewise survived. Their unique armour probably ensured that they filled a particular niche which could not be challenged. The crocodilians were the only archosaur reptiles to continue. They remain a familiar and sinister part of the aquatic fauna in many of the warmer parts of the world. Some species are today faced with extinction due to overhunting on the part of man. Although naturalists condemn such hunting, it is interesting that those who live in close proximity to the crocodiles and alligators do not complain about the decline in numbers. To them such a decline represents the demise of a potentially deadly threat. Conservation, at least in this instance, needs to be tempered by the demands of safety.

With the world cleared of dinosaurs and pterosaurs, there was plenty of scope for other types of animal to evolve and develop into the most important forms of life on Earth. One of the first to expand was yet another descendant of the archosaur group, the birds.

The exact ancestry of the birds is a matter of hot dispute amongst palaeontologists, those scientists who study extinct creatures. The earliest known bird fossil dates back around 150 million years and is known as *Archaeopteryx*. The skeleton of this animal clearly shows that it is descended from archosaurian forbears. Several features also indicate that it is closely related to various small carnivorous dinosaurs known collectively as coelurosaurs. These animals were small and lightly built predators which ran on their hind legs. The *Archaeopteryx* appears to have been a coelurosaur which gained excessively long arms to act as wings, and gained a covering of feathers.

However, some scientists, point out important differences between the skeletons of *Archaeopteryx* and contemporary coelurosaurs. They maintain that the birds descended from the archosaurs without passing through a dinosaur phase and believe that the immediate ancestors of the birds are yet to be discovered.

Whatever, the truth, the birds remained a minority group and very much in the background for many millions of years after the time of *Archaeopteryx*. However, before the extinction of the dinosaurs, the birds had spread out to become a very diverse and successful group of animals. There were birds specialised to diving for fish, birds adept at wading and some specialised for swift, agile flight.

Birds, as a group, have several features which give them a superiority over reptiles. Of these the most important are the feathers, which indicate two major advances. The first is the property generally known as warm-bloodedness. This means, simply, that birds maintain in interior heat which is kept steady no matter what the weather and temperature of the surrounding air. This enables the interior chemical reactions of the body to progress at steady, and therefore more efficient, rates.

The clear advantages of this feature are most obvious in cold climates, where birds can survive in areas which remain closed to reptiles. Elsewhere dawn brings lizards and other reptiles out to sun themselves and so raise their internal temperatures to get their bodies functioning properly. Birds, on the other hand, are already working at their most efficient rate and can hunt or feed while reptiles are getting going.

The second advantage indicated by the feathers is the power of flight. All modern reptiles are terrestrial, able to crawl or run but not to fly. Birds are therefore able to fly away from danger, fly towards food and undertake long migrations in search of seasonal feeding grounds. Such advantages were also enjoyed by the reptilian pterosaurs, but their wings were made up of flaps of leathery skin, in contrast with which wings of feathers posses several advantages.

Skin wings are highly vulnerable to damage. If a pterosaur brushed a bush or rock it might have torn its wing and so been incapable of flight until the wound healed. While earthbound it would have been an easy victim for any passing predator. Feathered wings, by contrast, can sustain quite high degrees of damage without becoming incapable of flight. If a feather is torn or broken the others remain unaffected and the bird can still fly. Further, feathered wings are more easily folded when not in use than large areas of skin. This has made birds more mobile on the ground and in trees than pterosaurs could ever have been. The development of strong, muscular legs increased this advantage to make birds more advanced than pterosaurs, which may account for the fact that pterosaurs were already dying out when the mass extinction of reptile groups occurred.

However, there have been some bird species which have abandoned the advantage of flight because local conditions make it redundant. Among the earliest to do so were the various species of *Diatryma* which lived in North America some 55 million years ago and stood over 7 feet in height. This powerful beast had tiny wings, quite incapable of flight, but powerful legs on which it could reach fairly high speeds. It ate seeds and fruits.

Much more formidable was the *Phororharcos* which lived 30 million years later in South America. This creature was a large predator which was well able to tackle any contemporary mammals with its taloned feet and savagely hooked beak.

Larger still were the moas of New Zealand which survived to within the age of history. These birds were most common on South Island where they were isolated from competition by mammalian plant-eaters and safe from attack by large predators. They were, therefore, able to grow to quite immense sizes. The largest, *Dinornis maximus*, stood about 11 feet tall and was a strict vegetarian.

The largest modern flightless bird is the ostrich, which inhabits the plains of central Africa and, like the moas, is a vegetarian. It stands about 9 feet tall and can achieve speeds of 45 miles per hour for short bursts. It uses this speed to escape from predators, but when cornered can inflict serious wounds with its clawed feet.

The only other significant group of flightless modern birds is the penguin of Antarctica. This specialised group of birds has adapted its wings to swimming rather than flight. The wings have become much smaller and stunted, but remained just as muscular. Using them as paddles penguins can move through the water at high speed in search of fish, or to escape the seals and whales which prey upon them. Like all birds, the aquatic penguins need to come to land to breed. They lay their eggs in large communal rookeries where many hundreds of breeding pairs gather each year for a few weeks to raise their young before returning to the seas in search of prey.

The majority of modern birds, however, do fly and are, therefore, rather light. The largest flying bird is the kori bustard of Africa which can reach weights approaching 50 pounds. Most birds are much smaller and some weigh only a few ounces. They are an immensely diverse group and include vegetarians as well as carnivores. Some are highly specialised. The hummingbirds, for instance, feed almost exclusively on nectar gathered from the year-round blooms of the tropical forests in which they live. Other birds have developed bills of specific shapes ideal for probing pine cones or scooping fish from the sea.

Birds of prey are generally good fliers and powerful birds, equipped with strong talons and hooked beaks, ideal for dealing with their victims. Some attack other birds, often striking at them in the air and clawing them from the sky. Others feed on small ground animals such as rodents and lizards. These birds hunt by cruising the air, watching the ground below for any sign of movement. When a victim is spotted, they fold their wings and drop, talons foremost, on to their prey.

Though so advanced, birds share one limiting factor with reptiles and amphibians. They lay eggs as part of their reproductive cycle. The egg, with its own food supply in the shape of the yolk and its sheltered environment for the developing embryo is a remarkably efficient means of reproduction. But it has one major disadvantage. If danger threatens the parents cannot flee with their eggs. They are forced either to fight to protect their offspring or to abandon it in the hope that camouflage will hide it from attack. All too often neither succeeds and the young fall victim to predators.

The mammals, however, have developed a much more efficient method of reproduction which ensures a higher survival rate. All mammals, apart from a few aberrant species, give birth to live young. The developing embryo is kept within the mother's body until it is old enough to survive in the outside world and is only then born. Parental care does not end with birth, but continues long after, for several years in some species. Mammals have mammary glands which secrete highly nutritious milk on which the young feed until they are capable of taking adult foods.

Two variations of this pattern have developed. In the first the young are born very early in development. They climb into protective pouches on its mothers' stomachs which contains mammary glands. The young animal remains in the pouch until it has grown much larger, but returns to the pouch whenever danger threatens, even when quite large and apparently able to look after itself. These pouched animals are known as marsupials and today survive mainly in Australia, though a few species are found in the Americas.

As the only indigenous mammals in Australia, the marsupials have evolved to fill all ecological niches open to them. The kangaroos are the large grazers of the open grasslands, and the wombats forest browsers. Tasmanian devils are small scavengers which have recently taken to hunting. The Tasmanian wolf, which may or may not be extinct, is a larger hunter capable of bringing down the biggest herbivorous marsupials.

The second type of birth pattern is known as placental. In this case the young stays in the womb much longer, nourished from the mother's blood system via the placenta. When it is born it is as developed as the marsupial is when it leaves the pouch. This system has important advantages over that of the marsupial and has given the placental mammals the edge in the struggle for survival. Wherever the two forms coincided, placental mammals have overcome the competition of the marsupials and driven them to extinction.

Placental mammals are today the dominant form of terrestial life. They include the largest and most important features of most faunas and have developed into a wide range of different forms and species. Among the herbivores are small rodents such as mice and voles, together with larger creatures such as deer and antelope. The largest land mammal of all is the 12 feet tall African elephant which follows its sedate path through the open savannah of the continent, despite its dwindling numbers.

Among the more formidable mammalian predators are the great cats, the lion and the tiger. Together the two species roam across most of Asia and Africa, preying on almost anything they care to attack. They are certainly able to tackle any of the plant-eaters which exist in their respective ranges, except the elephants, and even the young of these species can fall victim.

It may seem that the large mammalian predators are the pinnacle of the evolutionary scale. The mammals dominate all other groups, the amphibians, reptiles and birds, and the great cats are able to subdue most mammals, but there is one mammal which has proved itself to be even more successful than they. That is man. Armed with a superior intelligence and sensitive hands able to make and manipulate sophisticated tools, humans are able to tackle the world of wildlife, and to subdue it. Very few forms of animal can defeat man. Some, such as tigers, can become maneaters, but they are shot out of hand. Others, such as pigeons and mice, have learnt to live alongside man and to find sustenance in houses and towns. But man is able to control even these if he tries hard enough.

With his immense technological abilities, man is able to impose himself as the dominant creature on earth. Unfortunately the spread of human habitation is spelling doom for many species of animal. The passenger pigeon and dodo are among the many birds which have already been driven to extinction, and the Barbary lion and the quagga are among the mammals to share that fate. If man is to continue to enjoy the superb beauty of the world of wildlife he must learn to control his natural desires to expand and thrive. His ambitions must be tempered with consideration. For the world of wildlife is visibly shrinking.

The crocodilians are the closest living relatives of the long-extinct dinosaurs. Like their extinct cousins, the crocodilians are highly advanced reptiles, some species even caring for their young. Their hearts have separated ventricles and they are capable of standing on vertical legs for short periods. This improves their speed on land, but it is in the water that they hunt. Top: The American crocodile (*Crocodylus acutus*) is found in the southern United States and throughout Central America and is a huge beast, frequently reaching 20 feet in length. Remaining pictures: The American alligator (*Alligator mississipiensis*) is, at 12 feet, rather smaller but scarcely less powerful. It is restricted to swamps of the southern United States. Overleaf: The marsh mugger crocodile (*Crocodylus palustria*) of India and Sri Lanka.

Top left: A juvenile South African bullfrog (*Pyxicephalus adspersus*) eating a caterpillar. This large frog lives in underground burrows, but emerges at mating time to find its way to nearby ponds. Centre left: A European green treefrog (*Hyla arborea*). This small European amphibian is common in many southern parts of the continent and spends most of its time lurking in bushes and trees in wait for flying insects, which it catches with extraordinary skill. It is famed for laying over a thousand eggs at a time. Below: The golden arrow-poison frog (*Dendrobates auratus*) of Panama. As its name suggests this frog is used by local Indians as a source of poison for their arrows. The poison is contained in the skin and is a defence mechanism which deters predators. Bottom left: The ridged frog (*Ptychadena anchieta*). Bottom right: the common frog (*Rana temporaria*) which is found throughout Europe, except for parts of Spain. It is one the most familiar of European amphibians and is well known to gardeners who often find it in moist corners under stones or compost.

Above: The golden bell frog (*Litoria raniformis*). Above right: The horned frog (*Ceratophrys ornata*) of Argentina. This species grows to around 7 inches in length and hunts for invertebrates and small rodents among the leaf litter of the rainforest floor. The Colorado river toad (*Bufo alvarius*) belongs to the widespread toad family, species of which are found throughout the world, except in Australasia and in permafrost areas. It is a fairly slow-moving animal which lives further from water than many other amphibians. Below: The bullfrog (*Pyxicephalus flarigula*) consuming an entire mouse. Bullfrogs are the largest of the true frogs, growing up to 10 inches in length and are well able to prey on small mammals and reptiles. Below right: The red-eyed treefrog (*Agalychnis callidryas*) of Costa Rica. Tree frogs show special adaptations to a life in the trees. Their feet are expanded by special gripping discs to help the creature keep hold on leaves and twigs. Most species, however, need to return to the ground to seek out ponds in which to breed.

Right: The golden toad (*Bufo perglenis*) of the rain forests of Costa Rica. This beautiful animal has become increasingly rare in recent years and is now seriously endangered. Below: the arrow-poison frog (*Dendrobates lencomekes*), whose brightly marked skin is a warning to would-be predators that this creature has an unpleasant taste. The creature is well known because of the male's habit of carrying tadpoles from one pool of water to the next on its back. The eggs are laid in the pools of water which collect in hollows in trees, and need to be moved frequently. Below right: The edible frog (*Rana esculenta*), which is so dependent on water that it is rarely more than a few feet away from a pond or stream. Bottom left: A pair of common toads (*Bufo bufa*) in amplexus. This posture is used by all frogs and toads and is taken up only immediately prior to egg-laying. The pair swim together as the female releases her eggs and the male his sperm into the water. Bottom right: A square marked toad (*Bufo regularis*).

Right: the brightly marked poison dart frog (*Dendrobates pumilio*), with its bright red body and dark blue legs. These creatures move openly around the rain forests of Costa Rica without any apparent fear of predators. The bold markings which make these amphibians so visible are actually its best means of defence for it warns birds and reptiles of the poison contained in numerous skin glands. Below: The spadefoot toad (*Scapheopus sp.*) of the United States, which is specially adapted to life in dry areas, far from water. When the infrequent rains come, the spadefoots emerge from their burrows and gather in the short lived pools of water to breed. The tadpoles grow rapidly, even feeding on each other in their struggle to mature before the shrinking pools dry up completely. As soon as they are adult, the young frogs leave the water to excavate their own burrows. Below right: The American toad (*Bufo americanus*), which grows to around 3 inches in length and will eat any invertebrates it can catch. Bottom left: The moor frog (*Rana arvalis*). Bottom right: the Panamanian treefrog (*Hyla phaeota*).

These pages: One of the most notorious of all poisonous snakes, due to numerous Western movies, is the prairie rattler (*Crotalus viridis viridis*), one of 26 species of rattlesnake which inhabit the Americas. All rattlesnakes are poisonous and prey on any animal which is small enough to be swallowed whole. When approached by an animal larger than itself, such as a man or horse, the rattlesnake tends to move away, but if cornered it will use its rattle to warn the newcomer of danger. On hearing the ominous rattle, most creatures beat a hasty retreat for the bite of the rattlesnake is extremely painful and often fatal. The rattle itself is created by chambers of dead skin at the tip of the tail. These segments are created when the snake sheds its skin, which it does about once a year. The process begins when the skin turns opaque and separates from the fresh, new skin beneath. At this point (below left) the snake is temporarily blind. Before long most of the skin is shed (below) and the snake is capable of striking (facing page).

Below: A sidewinder (*Crotalus cerstes*) lurking in the sparse grass of the Sonoran Desert. This species is widespread throughout the arid areas of the American West where it hunts rodents and lizards. It is chiefly known for the curious tracks it leaves in the sand and which are often found at dawn, after the night-time forays of the snake. These marks consist of several parallel, slightly curved lines and are formed by the unique movement of this snake, which shifts itself sideways with a looping motion. Bottom left: A cottonmouth (*Agkistrodon piscivorus*) which inhabits freshwater habitats in the southern United States. The virulent poison of this snake is especially dangerous to man, and its notoriety has been increased by a popular country and western song. Bottom right: A Sonoran gopher snake (*Pituophis melanoleucus*), which gained its name from its habit of preying on gophers. Below right: An indigo snake from Florida. Right: A two-headed gopher snake. Facing page top: A western diamondback rattler (*Crotalus atrox*). Facing page bottom: A brown water-snake (*Natrix taxispilota*) devouring a catfish in the Florida Everglades.

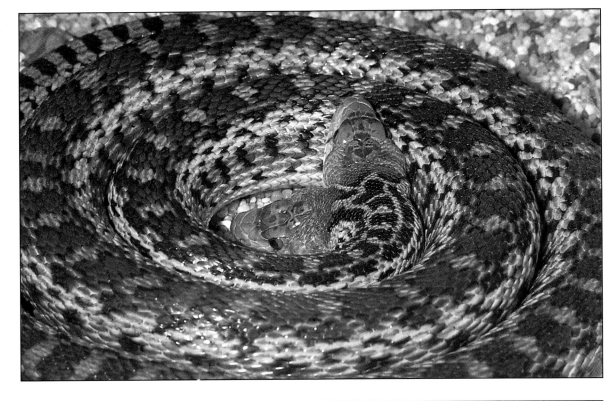

Left, below right and below left: The spitting cobra (*Nata pallida*) which is able to emit a stream of venom over distances up to eight feet. The spitting is a defensive mechanism which the cobra rarely employs, except when in immediate danger. The snake first rears up and takes visual aim at the eyes of the threatening creature. By constricting its poison sac violently, the venom is pushed forwards at high speed. If the venom strikes the eyes, it can be extremely painful and cause temporary blindness. In some cases permanent loss of sight can result, but immediate washing removes any such threat. The snake, meanwhile, has slunk away from danger. Bottom left: A gaboon viper (*Bitis gabonica*), which can reach 4 feet in length and has a highly toxic venom. It is, however, a slow moving creature and claims few human lives. Bottom right: An African rock python (*Python sebae*) devouring a rat. Pythons are non-venomous and kill their prey by constriction.

Right: A wandering garter snake moving through waterweed. Below: The king cobra (*Ophiophagus hannah*) shifting its grip to the head of a victim snake prior to swallowing it whole. The king cobra is the largest of the cobras, growing to a remarkable 18 feet, and the longest poisonous snake of all. It ranges widely through southeast Asia and, in common with other snakes, preys upon almost any animal it can catch. Below right: The startling hues of the yellow eyelash viper (*Bathriechis schlegelii*). This rather sluggish species comes in a variety of colours and has one of the most efficient venom fangs of all snakes. The fangs carry poison right to their tips and are hinged so that they can be folded back within the mouth when not in use. Bottom left: An indigo snake, showing signs of heavy tick infestation just behind its head. Bottom right: A carpet python (*Morelia argus*) climbs a tree in its native Queensland.

Right: A savannah monitor (*Varanus*) killing a spitting cobra. The savannah monitor is widespread on the grasslands of East Africa and, like other monitor lizards, is a powerful and adaptable reptile. It is able to swim strongly, to scurry quickly over open ground and to climb trees. It is also nimble enough to avoid the strikes of venomous snakes and, as here, to dart in to deliver the winning bite. Below: A male lasa lizard (*Tropidurus albemarlensis*) from the Galapagos islands where it has evolved in isolation for millions of years. Below right: The northern red salamander (*Pseudotriton ruber ruber*), which lives in damp regions of the northern United States where it feeds on earthworms and other invertebrates. Bottom left: A gecko (*Heteropholis poecilochlorus*), a genus of reptile peculiar to New Zealand. Some species of *Heteropholis* give birth to live young and are active during the day. Bottom right: A stump-tailed skink (*Tiliqua rugosa*) of South Australia in an impressive threat display.

Above left: The eyed lizard (*Lacerta lapida*), sometimes referred to as the jewelled lizard, gains both its common names from the series of blue and black roundels along its flanks. Common throughout southern Europe and North Africa, it grows to be over 2 feet in length and is extremely aggressive, tackling rats and snakes. Above: A young gecko hatchling (*Hemidactylus sp.*) newly emerged from its egg in Kenya. This genus is noted for the fact that its tail breaks off easily. This may be so that the lizard can escape pursuing hunters which have grabbed hold of its tail. The blood vessels within the stump close up almost immediately so as not to leave a tell-tale trail of blood. Left: The shingle-backed lizard (*Trachydosaurus rugosus*) of New South Wales. Bottom left: A forest dragon (*Gonocephalus boydii*) from Australia. Below: A rusty monitor (*Varanus*) rests on a dead branch in the Queensland mangrove swamps.

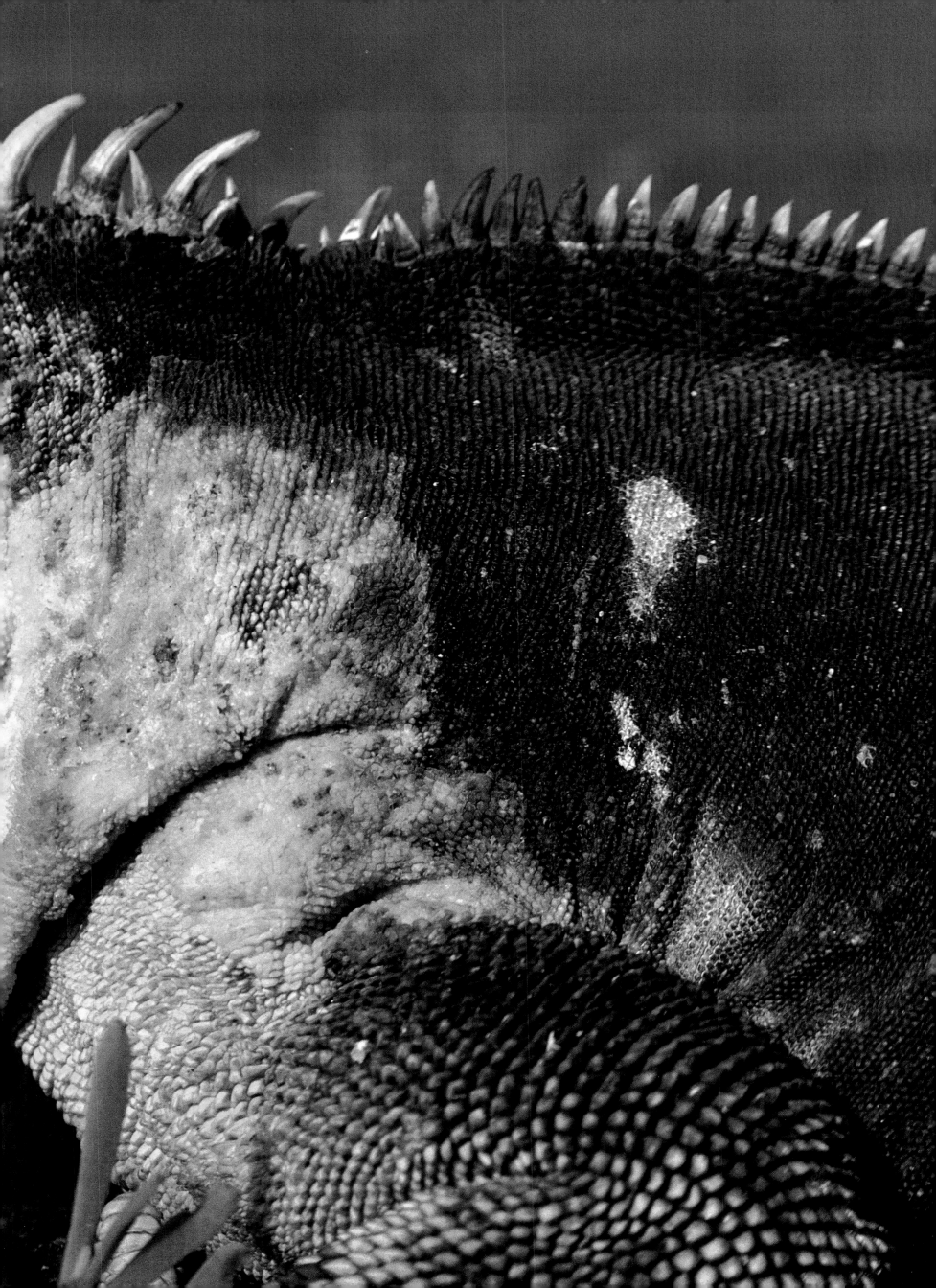

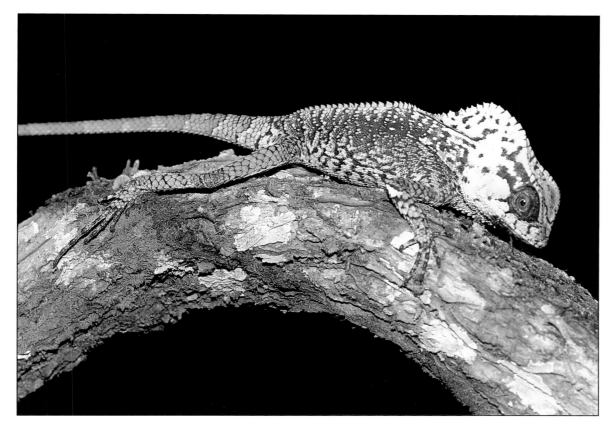

Facing page: There are over 400 species of iguana, but the type species is the true iguana (*Iguana iguana*) which can grow to over six feet in length and inhabit the tropical rain forests of South America. It is basically vegetarian, climbing through the branches of riverside trees to feed, and will readily drop into the water when alarmed. Left and below: The helmeted iguana (*Corytophanes cristatus*) from Costa Rica. Below left: The desert iguana (*Dipsosaurus dorsallis*) in the Mojave Desert. The iguanas gave their name to the very first dinosaur to be recognised by modern science. When fossils of a 30 foot long monster were found nobody knew what to make of them, but since the teeth resembled those of iguanas the creature was named *Iguanodon*, meaning 'iguana-tooth'. Bottom right: The marine iguana (*Amblyrhynchus cristatus*) of the Galapagos Islands is the only lizard to take to life in the sea. Bottom left: A chameleon preparing to strike at the insect hidden in the leaves.

Facing page: A bearded chameleon (*Chamaeleo hoehneli*) from Kenya, shown (top) striking at an insect on the wing and (bottom left) with its grotesque neck bulge. Left: A graceful chameleon (*Chamaeleo gracilis*) from Tanzania in the process of shedding its skin. Like many reptiles, chameleons shed their skin at periods to allow a new, larger skin to appear. Below left: A graceful chameleon rests on an isolated twig. Below centre: A female Fischer's chameleon (*Chamaeleo fischeri*) displaying the upturned nose horn and long tail for which this species is known. Below: A graceful chameleon devouring a grasshopper. Chameleon teeth are rather primitive and the process of chomping up prey can be rather untidy. Bottom right: A flap-necked chameleon (*Chamaeleo dilepis*) in one of the heavy downpours which periodically sweep tropical Africa where it lives. Bottom left: The impressive bearded dragon (*Amphibolurus barbatus*) of Queensland. This two foot long lizard is able to erect its neck pouch into an intimidating, spiked display when alarmed. This is usually enough to make a potential predator back off, but if not the dragon can run away with great speed.

These pages: The Jackson's chameleon (*Chamaeleo jacksonii*) is one of the most distinctive of all chameleons. The male (left, bottom right and facing page) has three horns facing forwards from its head. These are not weapons, but are used as threat displays between rival males during territorial disputes. The female (below and bottom left) has a small nasal horn, which is often all but invisible. Like all chameleons, Jackson's is specialised to a life hunting insects in trees. Its feet are specifically designed to grip twigs, with completely opposable toes. The creature moves with a distinctive swaying motion which blends in well with the movement of the background leaves and makes the lizard less conspicuous to potential prey. The chameleon is made even more inconspicuous by its ability to change colour. Special pigmentation cells can change the skin colour fairly rapidly in response to changing levels of illumination, though the skin colour can change in response to excitement levels, making the chameleon highly visible. It hunts by shooting out its extremely long, sticky tongue to swat insect prey.

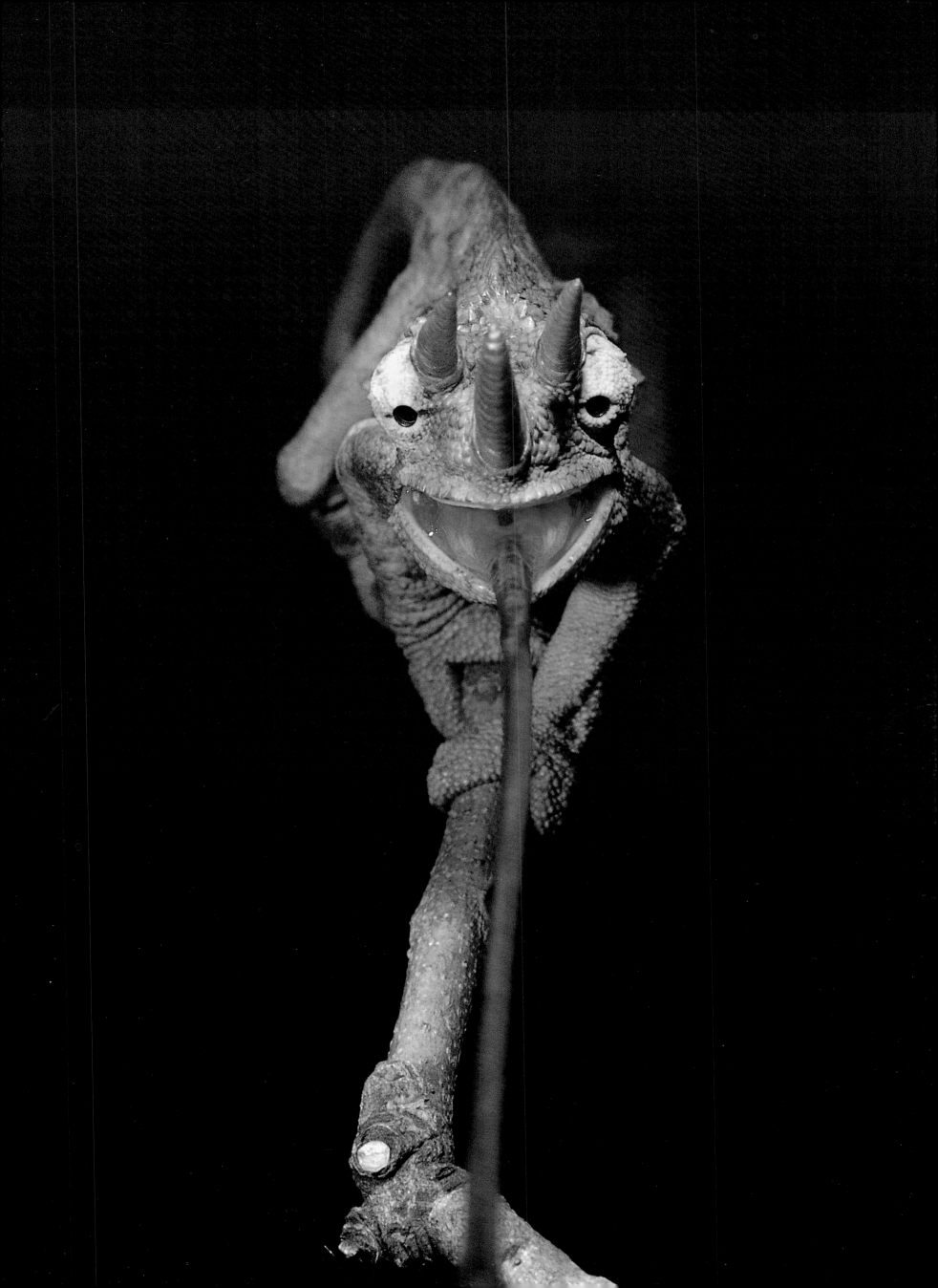

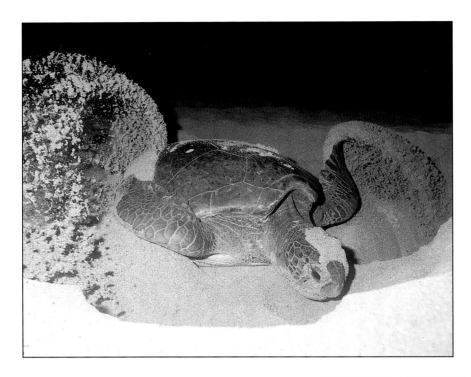

On land the heavy carapace of tortoises tends to slow the creature down and demands heavy, pillar-like legs to support its weight. Right: The Indian star tortoise (*Testudo elegans*) lives in the jungles of India and Sri Lanka, where it shelters in dense undergrowth during the day and ventures out to feed at night. The strikingly coloured Colombian species *Podocnemis cayanensis* (top right) has a similar lifestyle. Those chelions which have taken to an aquatic lifestyle, however, are freed from the crushing weight of their shell for the water supports it for them. As a result the green turtle (*Chelonia mydas*) (above) is able cruise the warm oceans worldwide at surprisingly high speeds. Though traversing huge distances, the green turtles return to specific beaches each year to breed. They lay their eggs in the sand and then abandon them, relying on the sun to incubate the eggs. Below: The three-toed terrapin (*Terrapin carolina tringuis*). Below right: The snapping turtle (*Chelydra serpentina*), which is found from southern Canada to Ecuador, attacking fish, birds and any other waterlife it can catch.

The giant tortoises of remote islands have been in danger of extinction for over fifty years. Though some local races have, indeed, died out, the majority are still in existence. Their numbers have in some cases risen recently, but are still only a fraction of their former maximum. When a ship put in to Rodrigues in 1691 the captain noted in his log that a herd of 3,000 tortoises was found just inland, and that one of his crew was able to travel 100 yards without touching the gound, but by stepping from one tortoise to the next. Such concentrations are no longer found. The tortoises are also known for their great age, though exactly how long one might live is unclear. One specimen lived 152 years after being captured, but it was already fully grown when caught and so may have been well over 200 years old when it died.

The sinister praying mantis (top) is a highly specialised insect which has evolved in the tropics to prey upon other insects. Its fore legs are long, muscular and spiny. At rest the limbs are tucked beneath the body, but when a victim comes within range the legs shoot out, to grasp the prey and hold it still while it is consumed. So successful is this pattern of hunting that over 2,000 species of praying mantis have evolved. Above left: The mormon cricket (*Anabrius simplex*) belongs to a large group of insects which are basically ground-living and are able to feed on almost any food which comes their way. Some species have become household pests. Above: The gila monster (*Heloderma suspectum*) lives in the southern United States and is the only poisonous lizard. Its bite is mild compared with that of snakes, but is effective against its small prey. Left: Clark's spiny lizard (*Sceloporus clarki*) from the Sonoran Desert.

Right: The fringe-toed lizard (*Uma notata*), which hunts its prey in the Sonoran Desert. Tortoises and turtles belong to the order Chelonia, one of the oldest groups of reptiles which dates back around 220 million years. The success of the group is shown by the way in which they have evolved to suit life on land, in the sea and in fresh water. The remarkable carapace which encases their entire bodies is probably the secret of their survival. Most species can withdraw into their shell, some being able to hide all vulnerable parts of the body from attack.
Below: The desert tortoise (*Gopherus agassizi*) which is adept at hiding in rock crevices.
Below right: The soft-shelled turtle (*Trionychidae*) of Florida lurks on the muddy bottom of streams and ponds, striking out with its supple neck to catch passing fish.
Bottom: The Florida red-bellied turtle (*Chryselius nelsonis*).

The various species of puffin (these pages) are amongst the most attractive and charming of sea birds. Hundreds of thousands of these birds inhabit the North Atlantic, feeding on fish and other marine animals. Puffins are extremely swift fliers and are able to dive using both wings and feet to power themselves while chasing prey. Top left: A tufted puffin (*Fratercula cirrhata*) emits its raucous 'arr' call, only rarely heard during the breeding season. Top right: A common puffin (*F. arctica*) displaying the vivid hues which its bill takes on during the breeding season. Above: A tufted puffin with a collection of dry grass which it is taking to its burrow to line the nest chamber. Left: A common puffin with a number of small fish in its bill. The bill is hinged so that the bird can snap up fresh prey while keeping a firm grip on those already caught. Facing page top: A group of common puffins. Facing page bottom: A horned puffin (*F. coraicuiata*) prepares to take off from its rocky perch in search of food.

The 86 species of kingfisher take their generic name from the European kingfisher (*Alcedo atthis*) (above and facing page) which has an attractive plumage of iridescent blue and green together with russet and white. This attractive bird hunts fish and other aquatic animals by perching on a branch overhanging a stream and diving down on any prey which swims within reach. Such behaviour is, however, unusual among kingfishers, most of which do not prey on fish at all. Instead, they hunt slugs, reptiles and other birds, though they have the short, stabbing bill of the European kingfisher. Top left: The rufous backed kingfisher (*Ceyx rufidorsus*) of Indonesia. Top right and left: The blue eared kingfisher (*Alcedo meninting*) of Java, one of the few tropical kingfishers to dive for fish. Centre: Africa's malachite kingfisher (*Alcedo cristata*).

Above: The hoatzin (*Opisthocomus hoazin*) which has been placed in a family all of its own. It frequents the densely wooded riverbanks of the Amazon basin, scrambling through the branches and showing a remarkably poor ability to fly. Top right: A pukeko (*Porphyrio porphyrio*) in New Zealand. Right: The ring-necked pheasant (*Phasianus colchicus*) of which over 50 localized races exist. Far right: The black korhaan of southern Africa. Below: The takahe (*Notornis mantelli*) of New Zealand, which was once thought to be extinct but is now known to survive in small numbers. Bottom right: A male sage grouse (*Centrocercus urophas*) of North America performing its elaborate and impressive courtship display. Facing page: A peacock (*Pavo cristatus*) resplendent in its iridescent blue neck plumage and startlingly coloured tail.

The birds of the North American deserts
inhabit a hostile environment where
temperatures soar to 120 degrees Fahrenheit
with blistering regularity. The birds feed on a
variety of foods, including cacti, seeds, insects
and small reptiles and mammals. Right: The
greater roadrunner (*Geococcyx californiana*)
which gained its name from its habit of
sprinting across open spaces, such as roads.
The gilded flicker (*Colaptes chrysoides*) makes
its nest in hollows in the larger cacti, where
its young will be safe from attack by snakes
and other land-based hunters. Bottom left:
The screech owl (*Otus asio*), which is found
throughout North America from Canada to
Mexico, hunts insects, reptiles and mammals
in the deserts but in moister environments
also takes frogs and other amphibians.
Bottom right: A summer tanager (*Piranga
rubra*), one of 240 species of brightly
coloured tanager in the New World. Below:
The brown-headed cowbird (*Molothrus ater*).

Hummingbirds are possibly the best fliers of all birds. They gained their common name from the constant hum set up by the rapid beats of their wings, often moving so fast that they appear blurred and indistinct. Beating their wings up to one hundred times each second, hummingbirds are able to hover or to move in any direction, even backwards. The reason for such amazing agility is that hummingbirds feed almost exclusively on nectar gained from flowers, and need to hover in front of the blooms while probing with their cylindrical tongue for food. The enormous amounts of energy expended by the birds in flight is replaced by the sugary nectar which they consume in large quantities. Because they rely on flowers, most of the 300 species of hummingbirds live in the tropical forests of South America where plants bloom throughout the year, though a few migrate further north during the summer.

Right: The brilliantly coloured yellow warbler (*Dendroica petechia*) of the Galapagos Islands. Below and below right: A male masked weaverbird (*Ploceus velatus*) building its elaborate nest in Namibia. Bottom left: A blue throated bee-eater (*Merops viridis*) with a catch on Java. Bottom right: A great tit (*Parus major*) which can be found throughout Europe, North Africa and southern Asia together with (right) the smaller coal tit (*P. ater*) which shares a similar range. Facing page top: The red-billed quelea (*Quelea quelea*) which inhabits much of sub-Saharan Africa, flying in flocks of up to a million individuals. It is probably the most numerous bird on earth. Facing page bottom: A meadow pipit (*Anthus pratensis*) feeding a juvenile cuckoo. The cuckoo is famous for its habit of laying eggs in the nests of other birds, and leaving the foster parents to care for the hatchling.

Those birds which remain resident in northern temperate forests throughout the year need to be able to find food even in the depths of winter. The birds (this page) find food during the British winter in a variety of ways. The bullfinch (*Pyrrhuyla pyrrhus*) eats seeds, but also consumes tree buds. The linnet (*Acanthis cannabina*) feeds exclusively on seeds, and some birds migrate to southern Europe. Right: The chaffinch (*Fingilla coelebs*) is possibly the most numerous British bird. During the winter it moves out of the woods and hedgerows to feed on stubblefields where it finds loose grain. Above: The robin (*Erithacus rubecula*) feeds on seeds, but will also take earthworms. Facing page top: The brownheaded cowbird (*Molothrus ater*) of the United States, like the cuckoo, lays its eggs in the nests of other birds. Facing page bottom: The jay (*Garrulus glandarius*) lives throughout Europe and much of Asia and North Africa, feeding on insects and berries.

The 25 species of bee-eater contained within the family Meropidae share the characteristics of a slightly downturned bill and an amazing ability to capture insects on the wing. In Africa, where most species are found, they are regarded as a friendly bird for they consume large numbers of locusts which would otherwise destroy crops. Above: The white fronted bee-eater (*Melittophaeus bullockoides*). Top right: Carmine bee-eaters. Both are communal birds which nest together in large colonies which may number over a thousand individuals. Above left: The related lilac-breasted roller (*Coracias caudala*) which inhabits East Africa where it takes small lizards in addition to insects. The brown-headed barbet (left) of Sri Lanka belongs to a large family of birds spread throughout the tropical areas of Africa, Asia and the Americas. It hunts insects, but also feeds on fruits, and is a solitary bird, except during the breeding season.

The toucans live in the dense canopy of South American rainforests. Their most extraordinary feature is the large bill, common to all species, which can be very brightly coloured. The purpose of this large protuberance remains obscure although it may be connected with visual displays during courtship. Left: The redbilled toucan (*Ramphastos tucanus*). Above left: The channelbilled toucan (*Cramphastos vitellinus*). The hornbills of Africa and Asia have similarly large bills and again their purpose remains unclear. The birds have a remarkable breeding pattern. First a suitable hole is found in a tree in which a nest is built. The female is then imprisoned in the nest by a wall of mud with a tiny hole, through which the male passes her food. The nest of the yellowbilled hornbill (*Tockus flavirostris*) (top right) has been cut away to show the structure. Top left: Van der Decken's hornbill (*Tockus deckeni*). Above: A wreathed hornbill (*Rhyticeros undulatus*).

The parrot family, which contains around 300 species, is spread throughout the tropics, though it is particularly common in South America and Australasia. Parrots are highly adapted to a life in trees, feeding on nuts, seeds and fungi. Their feet are strong and supple and can be used as 'hands' to manipulate food before eating. Equally characteristic is the upper bill which is linked to the skull by a hinge and can be used to remove seeds from husks or nuts from shells. The macaws are among the largest and most spectacular parrots, with colourful plumage and strident voices. Right: A pair of blue and yellow macaws (*Ara ararauna*), (bottom left) a scarlet macaw (*Ara macao*) and (facing page) the red and green macaw (*Ara chioroptera*). Below: The Redcrowned parakeet (*Cyanoramphus novaezelandise*). Below right: The rainbow parakeet of Australia. Bottom right: A salmoncrested cockatoo.

Owls are highly successful birds of prey which are widespread throughout the world and feed on small animals ranging in size from insects to rabbits. Part of their success is attributable to their silent flight, which enables them to take prey by surprise. The leading flight feathers of owls are narrow and loosely barbed producing an aerodynamic cushion. This disrupts the air-slicing effect of wings and so reduces noise. Right: an eagle owl (*Bubo bubo*) adopts a threatening attitude as the photographer approaches. Below: A long-eared owl(*Asio otus*). The conspicuous 'ears' have nothing to do with hearing, but are simply tufts of feathers. Below right: A Tengmalm's owl peers out from its nest. Bottom left: The watchful gaze of a great horned owl (*Bubo virginianus*). Bottom right: A barn owl (*Tyto alba*) perches on a wall after a successful hunt. Facing page: A great gray owl (*Strix nebutosa*) with its young.

The most noticeable feature of an owl's appearance is its face, with large eyes accentuated by the flat discs of feathers. Owls prey on small animals and frequently hunt at night or at dusk. Their eyesight is exceptionally keen to deal with poor visual conditions, while hearing also plays an important part in locating prey. Top left: a short-eared owl (*Asio flammeus*) from the Galapagos Islands. Top right: An eagle owl (*Bubo bubo*), the largest of all the owls with a wingspan of around five feet. Though found across Europe and central Asia, the eagle owl is restricted to forested areas where rocky slopes offer good nesting grounds. Above: A tawny owl (*Strix aluco*). The tawny owl is one of the most familiar European owls, hunting rodents and birds in open woodland and gardens. Right: A great gray owl (*Strix nebuiose*). Facing page: Pel's fishing owl with a catfish. Very few owls prey on fish, and those which do usually hunt more normal prey to supplement their diet.

The great white egret (*Egretta alba*) is one of the most elegant and spectacular birds of the heron family, the Ardeidae. It is distributed around the world, being divided into two subspecies. One race is common in the Americas, while the other ranges widely over Asia, Australasia and Africa. Only in Europe is the great white egret rare, being largely absent from much of the northern half of the continent. The bird has, for example, been sighted only three times in Britain since the First World War. Like all members of its family the great white egret preys on fish and aquatic invertebrates. Its favoured tactic is to stand motionless in shallow water, waiting for prey to swim within range of its stabbing bill. It will, however, sometimes stalk victims with slow, graceful strides through the water. The coloration of the egret's bill varies according to its breeding cycle. Out of season the bill is a bright yellow (left and below), but as the breeding season approaches it becomes darker and duller (remaining pictures) and sometimes becomes almost entirely black.

Top right and bottom right: The great blue heron (*Ardea herodias*) is a common American bird, wading through the wetlands in search of fish. It stands a little over three feet tall and is one of the continent's most elegant birds. Remaining pictures: The anhinga (*Anhinga anhinga*) is sometimes referred to as the snake bird because of its elongated, serpentine neck which ends in the long, stabbing beak. The anhinga hunts by diving in lakes and rivers in search of fish. It swims using its powerful legs, but keeps its wings firmly tucked by its side. The neck is kept coiled back while hunting, but will lash out to seize prey whenever possible. The bill is serrated for a better grip on slippery fish. The anhinga is a common sight throughout its range, which stretches from the southern United States to Argentina.

The wetlands of the southern United States, the Everglades and Mississippi Delta, form a haven for a large numbers of waterbirds, including those shown on these pages. The black-crowned night heron (*Nycticorax nycticorax*) lives up to its name by being mostly active at dawn and dusk, and being rarely seen in daylight hours. It is common throughout the Americas, as well as Asia and Europe and is probably the most common of all the herons and egrets. Top right, right and facing page top: The roseate spoonbill (*Ajaia ajaja*) is the only spoonbill to be found in the New World. The broad end of the bill contains a fine filter with which the bird can strain crustaceans from the water. Above: The white ibis which is closely related to the sacred ibis of Egypt. These birds were considered to be holy by the ancient Egyptians, who mummified their remains as a religious duty. Modern archaeologists have found thousands of these preserved birds. Facing page bottom: The cattle egret (*Ardeola ibis*) which feed on insects disturbed by grazing cattle.

There are five species of flamingo, grouped into three genera and a single family. The most common are the greater flamingo (*Phoenicopterus ruber*) (above left and top right) and the lesser flamingo (*Phoenicopterus minor*) (remaining pictures) both of which are found in Africa. Until a few years ago the flamingos were given their own separate order, but naturalists have now reclassified them as a family and grouped them in the order Ciconiiformes along with herons and storks. Like herons flamingos spend much of their time stalking slowly through shallow freshwater in search of food. The curious downturned bill of the flamingo is lined with fine hair-like structures which act as filters, removing tiny animals from the water. Flamingos are highly communal birds, gathering together in vast flocks of up to a million birds on the larger lakes. When startled the whole flock will lift off at once (above) in a magnificent display. They also breed together in large colonies, each pair constructing a mound of mud on which the eggs are laid (above left).

Geese are a widespread group of birds, which migrate between northern breeding grounds and southern wintering places. The snow goose (*Anser coerulescens*) breeds on the open tundra of Canada's Northwest Territories, where the short flush of summer growth provides food for the goslings (above), and moves south for the winter, (top) in South Dakota. Facing page top: Upland geese, Falkland Islands. Facing page bottom: Scaup (*Aythya novaeseelandiae*) in New Zealand.

Below: The mallard duck (*Anas platyrhynchos*) is one of the most widespread ducks of all, being numerous in the northern temperate lands. It breeds throughout its range, building a well camouflaged nest close to water. The wood duck (bottom right), as its name suggests, prefers lakes and streams in forests. Unlike most ducks, which nest on the ground, the wood duck lays its eggs in the hollows of trees. When the young hatch they must follow their mother to water. The majority of swan species are white, or nearly so. These include (right) the coscoroba swans (*Coscoroba coscoroba*) of South America, and (bottom left and facing page bottom) the trumpeter swan (*Cygnus buccinator*) of North America. So distinctive was this coloration that in medieval times the term 'black swan' was used to describe any piece of obvious nonsense. When early explorers returned from Australia to state that they had found a black swan they were rarely believed. However, such a bird does exist under the scientific name of *Cygnus atratus* (facing page top).

Grebes and divers are often grouped together, although the relationship between the two is rather uncertain. The grebes are freshwater birds which spend most of their time on the water. They build floating nests out of dead and decaying aquatic vegetation on which they lay their eggs. Left and facing page top: The great crested grebe (*Podiceps cristatus*) is found throughout the world, except for the Americas and is the largest grebe of all. The Slavonian grebe (*P. auritus*) is a smaller European species. The loons, or divers, are often found on coasts during the winter. Like grebes, they dive for fish, and are clumsy on land. Above: A Scottish red-throated diver (*Gavia stellata*). Top and facing page bottom: Arctic loons (*Gavia arctica*) nesting in Canada's Northwest Territories.

Top left: A pair of blue footed boobies (*Sula nebouxii*) which are restricted to the western coast of tropical America and various offshore islands. These birds gained their popular name from the startling blue feet and from their habit of wandering up to sailors, who promptly killed them and stored them as provisions. Top right: A light-mantled sooty albatross (*Phoebetria palpebrata*) with its chick on the island of South Georgia. Left and above centre: Nesting black browed albatrosses on the Falkland Islands. Albatrosses are famous for their flights, lasting many months without touching land. They stay airborne by using air currents and updrafts, swooping down to catch the fish and squid on which they feed. Above: A chick of the giant petrel calls raucously for its absent parents.

Below: A juvenile frigate bird momentarily abandoned by its parents. Frigate birds gained their name from the similarity between their behaviour and that of naval frigate ships during the days of sail. Naval frigates were swift, lightly armed warships which snapped up prizes. The frigate birds are similarly adept at robbing other birds of food, often attacking a gull in flight to force it to drop its prey. They are also superb fliers, effortlessly riding the air currents at will. This ability is largely due to the unsurpassed ratio of seven foot wingspan to three pound body weight. Right: A pair of king cormorants (*Phaladocorax albiventes*) in a breeding colony in Argentina. Unlike the frigate bird, the king cormorants remain in coastal waters. Bottom right: A small colony of Magellan blue-eyed shags, which are related to the cormorants and named for the Portuguese explorer of the Pacific Ocean. Bottom left: A southern giant petrel dives for food on South Georgia.

Above, top and facing page: The white pelican (*Pelecanus onocrotalus*) is one of the most successful fish-eating birds, a success largely due to its communal hunting behaviour. A group of perhaps two dozen birds will gather in a curved arc some distance offshore. The birds then begin to move forwards towards the shore, beating the water furiously with their wings, driving the fish before them. When the water is shallow enough for the birds to reach the fish, the formation breaks up as each bird dips its bill into the water to scoop up its meal. As the bird lifts its head, the water drains from its bill leaving the fish which are then swallowed. Right and above right: The brown pelican (*Pelecanus occidentalis*) hunts alone, diving into the water from a height of around 15 feet. Pelicans are among the oldest group of birds. Fossils of this genus have been found dating back 40 million years.

Right: The scientific name of the beautiful crowned crane (*Balearica regulorum*) derives from the fact that they were once found on the Balearic Islands of Minorca and Majorca. Today they are restricted to the plains of sub-Saharan Africa. Below: A male kori bustard (*Ardeotis kori*) displaying during the breeding season. The kori bustard lives on the plains of East Africa and is the largest of all the bustards measuring over four feet in length. Bottom right: The curious shoebill (*Balaeniceps rex*) which is placed in a family of its own. This bird lives in the swamps of central Africa and uses its huge bill to pluck frogs and fish from the mud. Top, far right and facing page: Ostriches (*Struthio camelus*), the largest living birds, which tip the scales at a massive 350 pounds and stand nine feet tall. The birds live in flocks on the open savannah of Africa, feeding on seeds and grasses and the odd insect or reptile.

The 18 species of penguin are superbly adapted to life in the water. They have lost the power of flight entirely, but their wings remain functional and power the birds through the cold Antarctic seas in search of fish. So unlike the normal bird are penguins that when they were first discovered by Europeans, scientists were uncertain whether they were birds at all. Facing page top: Emperor penguins (*Aptenodytes forteri*). Facing page bottom: King penguins (*Aptenodytes patagonica*). Above left: A fiordland crested penguin (*Eudyptes pachyrhychus*) with its down-covered chick. Above: A Magellan penguin (*Spheniscus magellanicus*) on the Falkland Islands. Left: A macaroni penguin (*Eudyptes chrysolophus*) sporting its curious eyebrow tufts. Below left: A breeding colony of emperor penguins, with the chicks huddled against their parents for warmth. Below: A gentoo penguin (*Pygoscelis papua*) and its young.

Penguins are typically Antarctic creatures, spending most of their lives cruising the chill southern waters in search of fish and squid. The birds derive all their power from their wings, which have evolved into paddles, useless for flight. The larger species, such as the king penguin, shown (facing page) on South Georgia, are among the best insulated against the cold and spend more time in the extreme south than smaller species such as those on this page. Right: The rockhopper penguins (*Eudyptes crestatus*) follow each other on a typically rock-hopping journey along the coast of the Falklands. These birds often build their communal nesting sites some distance from the sea and need to trek to them after each fishing trip. Below: A chinstrap penguin (*Pygoscelis antarctica*) feeding its month-old chick. Below right and bottom: A colony of adelie penguins (*Pygoscelis adeliae*).

The vast majority of modern penguins are around two feet in height, with only the emperor penguin topping three feet. Five million years ago, however, a species of penguin existed which stood over five feet. Like most prehistoric giants, the giant penguin died out leaving smaller members of its type to survive. The gentoo penguins breed on the Falkland Islands, where large colonies are established for the breeding season. At first the young chick is covered in soft down (right) to protect it against the chill winds. Later the down is moulted and replaced with the sleek, water-proof feathers of the adult (facing page). Top: A long procession of chinstrap penguins moving from the breeding colony to the sea to fish. Parents take turns at guarding the chick while their mates feed. Above: A lone rockhopper penguin on New Island, one of the more remote Falklands.

These pages: The magnificent bird of prey, the bald eagle (*Haliaeetus leucocephalus*), which has become famous as the national symbol of the United States of America. It was once common throughout North America but is now very restricted in range, being found only in Alaska and in the more remote areas. Measuring up to 40 inches in length, this is a powerful bird, armed with strong talons and a wickedly hooked beak. Despite this it feeds chiefly on carrion, taking dead fish from lake shores or from the river surface where they float. The summer salmon run of the Pacific Coast, when thousands of large salmon die in mountain streams is a particularly abundant time for bald eagles. When such easy prey is absent, however, the bald eagle will take live fish, swooping down from the sky to plunge talon-first into the water and emerging with a catch. It will then fly to a nearby perch to devour is prey (bottom right and facing page). Below and below right: Bald eagles breed annually, producing two chicks, yet few chicks survive to adulthood and the reproduction rate is low, making it difficult for this bird to re-establish its numbers.

Top: The Arctic tern (*Sterna paradisaea*) is famous for its extraordinarily long migration route, the longest of any animal in the world. They breed during the northern summer along the coasts of Greenland and North America. As soon as the chicks are old enough to fly, the terns cruise southeastwards towards Europe and then coast south along Africa to the Cape of Good Hope and beyond. This bird was photographed near the sea ice of Antarctica. Terns breeding in northern Russia head for Australia on an equally daunting annual flight. The brown-headed gull, photographed (above) on Teilkland Island, has its distinctive head colour during the breeding season only, reverting to white soon after. Above right: The herring gull (*Larus argentatus*), the commonest gull in northern Europe. Right: Great black-backed gulls (*Larus marinus*) with their chick. Facing page: Grey-headed gulls (*Larus cirrocephalus*) rest.

Above: A pair of red-billed gulls (*Larus suopulinus*) rest in the weird setting of Rotorua, New Zealand, where billowing clouds of steam well up from deep within the earth. Above right: A graceful Antarctic tern on the wing. Right: A black-headed gull (*Larus ridibundus*) carrying a morsel of food from the sea. The misleading common name of this bird describes its breeding plumage. Throughout most of the year it is, as shown here, coloured in shades of white and grey. Below: A black skimmer (*Rynchops nigra*) feeding off the coast of Texas. This bird is widespread along the coasts of both Americas and has a unique feeding pattern. It flies at high speed, just above the water surface with its lower bill cutting through the surface. When the bill strikes a fish the bird snaps its mouth shut and swallows its catch instantly. Bottom right: A Caspian tern (*Sterna caspia*) on its nest near San Francisco, California. Facing page top: An Arctic tern. Facing page bottom: A pair of four-week-old greater black-backed gulls.

The eagles, classed in the family Accipitrinae, are the most majestic and powerful birds of prey. Facing page: The ornate hawk eagle (*Spizaetus ornatus*) of South America. Top: The martial eagle (*Volemaetus bellicosus*) which hunts in southwestern Africa. Left: A bataleur eagle. Above: A hoatzin chick hangs precariously from a riverside branch. These chicks have small claws on their wings to aid them in climbing, a feature which is found on no other modern bird but which was characteristic of birds 150 million years ago.

Facing page: The remarkable markings of the king vulture (*Sarcorhamphus papa*), a native of Central and South America. The purpose of the colourful head features is unclear, but as they do not develop until the bird is fully adult, they may be connected with courtship. This bird inhabits the tropical forests of its range and is therefore unable to use the sharp eyesight of other vultures in its search for carrion. Instead it relies on scent to find the flesh of dead animals. Hardly surprisingly, dead fish form a large part of its diet. This page: The African fish eagle (*Haliaeetus vocifer*) is also heavily dependent on fish. This bird is a close relative of the American bald eagle and shares its white head and tail. It is particularly common in the lakes and swamps of central and southern Africa where it hunts for live fish, as well as taking carrion.

Left: An osprey (*Pandeion haliaetus*), one of the most beautiful birds of prey, spreads its wings to protect its young from the searing heat of the noon day sun. Below left: A juvenile merlin (*Falco columbarius*) and (below) an adult female. These birds are small for predators, measuring just 10 inches in length, but they are highly successful hunters. The bulk of their prey is made up of smaller birds, which they follow with a swift, agile flight. Bottom left: A buzzard (*Buteo buteo*), a powerful hunter of open woodland takes to the air in search of prey. Bottom right: A sparrow-hawk (*Accipiter nisus*) devouring a starling. The sparrow-hawk is widespread throughout Europe and northern Asia, although its numbers have been reduced by gamekeepers resentful of the bird's habit of taking young pheasants. Facing page: A goshawk (*Accipiter gentilis*) is like a large sparrow-hawk, and belongs to the same genus.

Facing page: A juvenile hen-harrier (*Circus cyaneus*) remains in its nest as it moults its down in favour of adult flying feathers. Top left: The ominous appearance of a Harris hawk as it studies the Sonoran Desert for prey. Top right: A buzzard (*Buteo buteo*) on a kill. Buzzards are widespread throughout North America, Europe and northern Asia where they prey upon rodents, carrion and other birds, but will not scorn smaller prey such as insects and worms. Above left: The crested caracara (*Polyborus plancus*) of Mexico which feeds mainly on carrion and will not hesitate to drive other scavengers away from a carcass. Above: A female kestrel (*Falco tinnunculus*) with a starling, a prey it takes most often in towns. Country kestrels prefer to feed on rodents and the larger insects. Left: A male peregrine falcon, which is found on every continent except South America. It has a dramatic hunting technique, plummeting down from a great height on to flying birds.

Right and facing page: Easily the most impressive of the birds of prey is the golden eagle (*Aquila chrysaetos*) which is to be found in mountainous regions throughout Asia, Europe and North America. It hunts by cruising at high altitude, scanning the ground for prey. When a victim is spotted, the bird folds its wings and plummets down with outstretched talons at speeds approaching 100 mph. It preys on hares, grouse, lambs and other small animals. Several reports speak of golden eagles carrying off human babies and toddlers, though these are rare occurrences. Below: The short-toed eagle devouring a grass snake. Most birds of prey use their talons to hold down prey while tearing flesh with their hooked beak. Below right and bottom left: A white-bellied sea-eagle (*Haliaeetus leucogaster*) which hunts the lakes and streams of Sri Lanka. Bottom right: The Brahminy kite (*Haliastur indus indus*), which is found in India and is particularly common in Australia.

The powerful grizzly bear (these pages) was formerly given its own species name of *Ursus horribilis*, but it is now generally reckoned to be a sub-species of the brown bear and is referred to as *Ursus arctos horribilis*. The change of classification has not altered the beast's position as the biggest and most powerful bear on the American continent. It has been known to attack animals as large as horses and, on at least two recent occassions, has taken to maneating. The bear finds most of its food among less formidable sources. It will enjoy fruits, nuts and even grass, as well as attacking rodents and other small mammals. During the spring thousands of salmon run up the Pacific streams to breed and the grizzlies move in eagerly to take their pickings. The bears often eat only the tastiest part of the fish, leaving the rest to be picked clean by gulls and carrion-eaters.

The grizzly bear (right, below, below right, bottom left and facing page) was once widespread across the entire North American continent, living in the Appalachian forests and on the plains as well as in the northern and western forests generally thought of as its home. European settlers found the presence of such a large and aggressive animal so close to their homes to be intolerable and ruthlessly hunted it to extinction. Today the grizzly is numerous only in Alaska and neighbouring areas of British Columbia and the Northwest Territories, though a few are found in the Rocky Mountains. In these chilly areas the bears den up for the winter, though they do not practice true hibernation. Bottom right: The Kodiak bear (*Ursus arctos middendorffi*) is larger than the grizzly, reaching 13 feet tall when it rears on its hind legs. It is confined to Kodiak Island, off the southern coast of Alaska, where it feeds almost exclusively on plants.

These pages: The brown bear (*Ursus arctos*) is the most widespread and common of all the bears. It is to be found in the more remote parts of Europe, throughout northern Asia and across much of North America, though it has been driven from large areas of its range by the spread of agriculture. As might be expected with such a broad distribution, there are numerous sub-species of which the grizzly bear is the most famous. Despite their name, various sub-species range in colour from yellow to near-black as well as varying shades of brown. Through most of the year the brown bear is a solitary animal, finding its food deep in forests. In the spring the bears pair up for mating, before separating again. The cubs are born in the winter, when the mother has denned up against the cold. By the time the warm weather returns the cubs are old enough to follow their mother.

Like most species of bear the American black bear (*Ursus americanus*) has a wide ranging diet consisting of both plant and animal food. They will eagerly devour fruit, nuts and roots and will hunt for small mammals and fish. They will also take carrion, seeking it out with their remarkably acute sense of smell. The black bear (facing page top) has come across a deer carcass floating downstream and dragged it to the riverbank. From there it pulled it inland and devoured the choicest pieces, leaving only bones and sinew (below). During the autumn the woods become rich with berries and fruits, of which the bears eat prodigious quantities. Thick reserves of fat build up beneath the skin as autumn turns to winter, and the bears find a secure cave or hollow in which they can build a den to protect themselves from the winter weather.

Facing page top: A bull elk (*Cervus canadensis*) gazes across the frosty Canadian plains. The impressive antlers of the bull elk grow afresh each year and can be 5 feet in length. They are used in courtship battles and, unlike fights among most other species, such fights can result in serious injury or death. The females (above left) do not grow antlers, and remain wary of intruders, especially when accompanied by young. The largest deer of all is the moose (*Alces alces*), known in Europe as the elk, which can stand over 6 feet at the shoulder. Unlike other deer, the moose is a solitary animal and spends much of its time in lakes and ponds. Top left: An adult mule deer (*Odocolleus hemionus*), which gained its popular name from the large, mule-like ears which it possesses. Top right: A pair of mule deer fawns, whose spotted coat blends in well with the dappled light of the forest floor. Above: The pronghorn (*Antilocapra americana*), the only surviving species of a once numerous group

Facing page top: The American elk (*Cervus canadensis*), or wapiti, which many believe to be identical with the European red deer (*Cervus elaphus*) rather than a distinct species. Facing page bottom: A reindeer (*Rangifer tarandus*) moves across the bare landscape of South Georgia, an isolated island close to Antarctica. The reindeer, or caribou, is native to the tundra of Canada and northern Europe, but was introduced to South Georgia by man to serve as a source of food. Left: a male bighorn sheep (*Ovis canadensis*) of the Canadian mountains which uses its impressive horns in head-butting contests during the rutting season. Bottom right: A pair of bighorn sheep lambs. Below: The chital (*Axis axis*), or spotted deer, of India which is a favourite prey of the tiger. Below centre: A female Rocky Mountain goat (*Oreamnos americanus*) and its kid high in the range from which it takes its name. Bottom left: a herd of dall sheep (*Ovis*) in the Yukon.

Top left: The European fox (*Vulpes vulpes*) is one of the most successful of all dogs. It is a nocturnal hunter, preying on birds, small mammals, invertebrates and even fish. Its adaptability has allowed it to survive alongside man. The female vixen gives birth to young inside the earth during the spring when food is plentiful. The cubs, (above) at 4 weeks and (right) at 3 months, stay near the den site until they are nearly grown. Top right: The gray fox (*Urocyon cinereoargenteus*) is a common American species which is to be found as far north as the Great Lakes and southward to Venezuela and is unusual among dogs for its tree-climbing ability. This individual was photographed in Florida. Above right: A Patagonian fox (*Dusicyon griseus*). Facing page top: The Cape fox of southern Africa. Facing page bottom: A coyote (*Canis latrans*) which hunts small animals on the American plains.

Facing page top: A pack of spotted hyenas (*Crocuta crocuta*) squabbling with vultures for possession of a buffalo carcass on the East African plains. Hyenas are famed as cowardly scavengers. This reputation has grown up because they scavenge during the day and hunt only at night when they are not so easily observed. Modern research indicates that hyenas gain most of their food by nocturnal hunting. Facing page bottom and bottom: The coyote (*Canis latrans*) which is highly adaptable and has invaded some urban areas where it feeds on food scraps. Below left: The wolf, one of the most widespread of the wild dogs, hunts in packs with each individual co-operating with the others. Because of their liking for domestic stock, wolves have been exterminated by man from large areas of Europe and North America. Below: The silver-backed jackal of East Africa. Left: The bat-eared fox (*Otocyon megalotis*) of southwestern Africa.

Because man is a member of the primate group, these creatures are often considered to be among the most advanced mammals, their very name means 'first'. In fact primates are very unspecialized, retaining five digits on each limb and having a full complement of teeth. The lemurs are among the most primitive, appearing more like insectivores than advanced primates. Bottom left: The black lemur (*Lemur macaco*) lives in dense forests on Madagascar, the island to which all lemurs are restricted. Monkeys, by contrast, are the most advanced primates, next to man. Right, below and below right: the yellow baboon (*Papio*), like other baboons, has evolved to a life on the ground on the open savannahs of Central Africa. Bottom right: The woolly monkey (*Lagothrix lagothrix*) which inhabits the forests of Peru and the western area of the Amazon Basin.

Monkeys are divided into two main groups the Cebidae, or New World monkeys, and the Cercopithecidae, or Old World Monkeys. New World monkeys have dense fur, but bare faces and possess a prehensile tail which can be used as an aid in climbing. Left: The white-faced saki monkey (*Pithecia*) which searches for fruit in the Amazon forests. Bottom left: Dourocouli (*Aotus trivirgatus*), otherwise known as the night monkey. Dourocolis are catholic in their diet, taking fruit, insects and small mammals as they move through the trees at night. Bottom right: The red-faced uakari (*Cacajao rubicundus*), which blushes when excited. Below: An Old World monkey, the vervet (*ICercopithecus aethiops*).

The orang utan (*Pongo pygmaeus*) is native to the coastal forests of Borneo and Sumatra. Some authorities see the two islands as supporting distinct subspecies of the ape, though this is not definite. It is accepted, however, that this animal is endangered. The felling of the lowland forests in recent years to provide farmland for the booming Indonesian population has led to a loss of habitat. The name of the ape is local dialect for 'old man of the woods' and the orang utan's appearance can be very human with its flat face and beard. The apes live singly, or in pairs, moving through the trees by swinging from branch to branch in search of the fruit, seeds and eggs which they eat.

The largest of all the apes is the gorilla. Adult males, referred to as silverbacks because their grey hairs, can stand over 6 feet in height, and weigh well in excess of 450 pounds. They are immensely powerful animals and, when provoked, are capable of inflicting much damage. They are, however, generally content to lead a fairly quiet life, moving through the dense bamboo thickets where they live. Gorillas exist in family groups of around twenty or so individuals, lead by a dominant, adult male. They feed on bamboo and other forest plants, and never take animal flesh. There are three distinct sub-species of which the mountain gorilla (*Gorilla gorilla beringei*) (facing page top) is the rarest. The eastern lowland gorilla (*G. gorilla graueri*) (remaining pictures) is more numerous, but is still an endangered animal. The western gorilla (*G. gorilla gorilla*) is the type subspecies.

The armadillos are a remarkable group of animals, being the only mammals to develop bony armour. The carapace of the armadillos is made up of bone plates overgrown by a horny substance. Solid sheets of armour cover the creature's shoulders and rear, but flexible bands separate the two enabling the armadillo to roll up into a virtually impregnable ball. Armadillos are also powerful diggers which excavate extensive living burrows, or can bury themselves away from danger. Top left and right: The nine-banded armadillo (*Dasypus novemcinctus*) grows to nearly three feet in length and is the only species to live in North America. Above: The giant armadillo (*Priodontes giganteus*) is the largest armadillo, reaching almost 5 feet in length. The hairy armadillo (*Chaetophractus villosus*) is limited to the plains of Argentina. Top right: The cape pangolin (*Manis temmincki*) has a covering of tough, sharp scales formed of specialised hairs.

Anteaters form a distinct group of mammals specialised to preying on termites, ants and other communal insects. They are all equipped with strong digging claws to excavate the insect nests and with a long, sticky tongue with which to collect their prey. Left: The giant anteater (*Myrmecophaga jubata*) can grow to over eight feet in length. Bottom left: The tamandua anteater (*Tamandua tetradactyla*) is a good climber, finding prey in the canopy of the Amazon rain forest. Bottom right: The two-toed anteater (*Cyclopes didactylus*) which is highly secretive and whose habits remain uncertain. Below: The aardvark (*Orycteropus caffer*), which is unrelated to anteaters but has a similar lifestyle. Below left: The Virginian opossum (*Didelphis virginiana*) which, when threatened, will lie still and imitate death, literally 'playing possum'. Most predators lose interest when the opossum does not make any attempt to flee.

The sloths are reputed to be the slowest mammals on Earth, a reputation they richly deserve. They hang from branches in the South American forests, moving slowly to find fruit and leaves. The sloth is not particularly fussy about its food, eating whatever vegetation comes within reach. Top left: The two toed sloth (*Choloepus didactylus*) is restricted to Brazil and, as its name suggests, has two toes on its fore feet. Above and top right: The three toed sloth (*Bradypus tridactylis*) ranges more widely, reaching as far north as Central America. Facing page and above right: The brush-tailed possum from Australia. This small mammal is a good climber, scurrying through the trees in search of fruit, leaves and insects. Like other possums it is a marsupial. The similar woolly opossum (*Caluromys laniger*) of Panama belongs to the only group of marsupials to be found outside of Australasia.

Marsupials are a group of animals entirely different from the majority of mammals. They give birth to young while they are very poorly developed and care for them in a pouch on the abdomen. Marsupials once lived throughout the world, but competition has pushed them to extinction on most continents. Only in Australia have marsupials continued to flourish and exist in many different species. Right and bottom left: The koala (*Phascolarctos cinereus*) is extremely attractive and has inspired many children's toys. The grey kangaroo (*macropus giganteus*) roams across much of eastern and southern Australia, grazing on the plentiful grass. It moves by hopping on its powerful hind legs and can achieve speeds of up to 30 miles per hour and clearing obstacles over ten feet in height. Similar, but rather smaller are the wallabies, of which the red-necked wallaby (*Macropus rufogrisea*) is the most common.

The giant panda (*Ailuropoda melanoleuca*) is one of the most appealing animals on earth. Its rounded profile and curious markings have made it popular with the public and with soft toy manufacturers. It is, however, very rare and has been adopted by the World Wildlife Fund as their symbol. Exactly how rare the giant panda is has become a subject of much controversy. Some naturalists believe that the creature is close to extinction while others maintain that the panda survives in viable breeding numbers. The confusion arises out of the secretive habits of the creature. It lives high in the remote mountains of central China amid vast dense forests of bamboo. Humans rarely venture into the bamboo thickets and so encounter pandas infrequently. Throughout most of the year the panda is a solitary animal, shunning company and so making an accurate assessment of population figures even more difficult. Most people agree, however, that the panda is worth saving.

Until a few hundred thousand years ago the elephant family was spread across every continent except Australia and Antarctica and was represented by dozens of types of of mammoth, mastodon and other genus. Today, the elephant family is reduced to just two species, the African and the Indian. Facing page top: The African elephant (*Loxodonta africana*) is the larger of the two, standing up to 12 feet tall. It is at home on plains and open forest where it feeds on grass and leaves. The numbers of African elephants have declined steeply in recent years due to illegal and large-scale poaching in supposedly protected areas. Remaining pictures: The slightly smaller Indian elephant (*Elephas maximus*) has also reduced in numbers recently due to loss of habitat rather than hunting.

These pages: The leopard (*Panthera pardus*) is possibly the most successful of all the big cats. It is to be found throughout Africa, and across much of Asia from Turkey through to Manchuria and southern Siberia. Its coat has beautiful markings of gold and black, with the black spots being collected together in roseates on the back and flanks. In some areas entirely black individuals occur and are referred to as black panthers. They are, however, merely black leopards, and in some lights the roseates are visible. Leopards hunt a wide range of prey, taking virtually any animal which they are strong enough to subdue. The cat does, however, have an unfortunate taste for dogs and it is the search for dogs which takes leopards into country villages where they encounter man. Several leopards have taken to maneating after such a visit, killing dozens of humans before they are shot. Usually, however, the wary leopard is rarely seen and taking accurate census of these animals is notoriously difficult.

These pages: The cheetah (*Acinonyx jubatus*) is the ultimate hunter of the plains. It is able to achieve speeds approaching 70 miles per hour as it pursues equally fleet-footed prey across the open grasslands of Africa. The cat is able to achieve these high speeds because its long, muscular legs have a tremendous reach, increased by the supple back which can arch and bow to extend the stride. Usually hunting alone, cheetahs prefer to stalk small antelope, rodents and birds and then to make a final dash for the kill. The victim may then be dragged into cover (above and top) before being devoured. When family groups co-operate in the hunt, cheetahs can run down prey as large as the largest antelope to provide a meal for all (facing page top). Right: The care and training of the cubs is the sole responsibility of the mother, with whom they stay until they are aged about 2 years.

Lions (*Panthera leo*) are among the most communal of cats, and the care of the young is a duty shared by the whole pride. Mating (above) may take place at any time of year and the cubs are born fully furred and with their eyes open. While young, that (top left) is 2 months old, cubs are kept away from the hunt by the male lions, who protect them from jackals and hyenas. As further protection cubs have mottled markings on their legs and flanks which serve to break up their outline and make it merge with the dry grass of the savannah. Once they have been weaned at about 6 months (facing page) the cubs are allowed to gather around a kill, though they are forced to eat last. Only as they reach maturity do the young take an active role in the hunt and assume their full place in pride hierarchy. This social system is seen most clearly after a kill. the hunting lionesses will give place to the lions who feed first, taking the best pieces.

The lion (*Panthera leo*) was once far more widely distributed than it is today, but the activities of man has forced it to retreat to areas where wild big game is still available. Lions were to be found in Greece as recently as 3,000 years ago and in the Middle East much more recently. The large Barbary lion of North Africa and Cape lion of South Africa were exterminated about a century ago, while the diminutive Mesopotamian race vanished some years earlier. The Indian lion, a small race, was nearly exterminated in the years immediately before World War I, but a vigorous conservation plan has raised their numbers to a few hundred. Only in East Africa does the lion remain numerous.

Lions live together in prides, which consist of one or two dominant adult males and perhaps half a dozen females together with juveniles. They owe much of their hunting success to co-operation for though they are powerful beasts, they are neither fast nor agile. A typical hunting pattern might involve a pair of lionesses moving upwind of a herd of zebra to start the quarry moving. They are then able to identify any weak or wounded animal and to concentrate on it. The intended victim is then carefully driven towards cover where the rest of the pride is waiting. As soon as the waiting lionesses feel they stand a chance of reaching their victim, the trap is sprung with each individual seeking a kill. Once a victim has been brought down (top left and above right) the lioness waits for the pride to gather for the feast. Lone males hunt for themselves, usually concentrating on smaller prey, (above) a lion with a springbok. Between hunts the pride rests (remaining pictures).

The tiger (*Panthera tigris*) is the most majestic predator of Asia, and the largest cat of all. There are several localised races of tiger, of which the largest is the Siberian tiger which can reach a length in excess of 10 feet. The smallest is the Javan, which may be extinct and which rarely tops 6 feet. The most numerous race is the Bengal tiger (right, below right, bottom left, bottom right and facing page) which inhabits wilderness areas of the Indian subcontinent. At the beginning of this century there were about 40,000 Bengal tigers, but destruction of habitat and hunting have reduced this to around 2,000. Vigorous government action has established national parks and made tigers a protected species. Population figures seem to be increasing, but problems with maneating has led to calls for renewed hunting. Below: The leopard (*Pantera pardus*) is widespread throughout Asia and Africa and is a successful hunter which relies on stealth to capture its victims.

Though the horse first evolved in North America several million years ago, the truly wild species of horse survive only in Africa and Asia. In Africa zebras and asses roam the plains while in Asia small numbers of Przewalski's horse still run free. Far more numerous is the Asiatic wild ass (*Equus hemionus*) (top left) which ranges between the Lebanon and Mongolia. These small wild horses frequent regions of sparse grazing, such as desert fringes and mountain meadows, where man has not led his flocks. There are several distinct races of Asiatic wild ass of which the khur, shown here, was numbered in the thousands as recently as the 1950s. Unfortunately, a catastrophic disease seriously reduced its numbers, though populations are presently recovering. Many areas are now the home to herds of domestic horse run wild. These animals quickly revert to the natural lifestyle of small herds dominated by stallions, but maintain the physical characteristics of the domestic horse. In America such creatures are known as mustangs (above, above left, left and facing page) and run alongside wild donkeys.

Facing page: Yaks (*Bos mutus*) are the wild cattle of Asia and once roamed across the Himalayan massif from northern India to western China. They are now restricted to the more inaccessible valleys and mountain pastures where they are able to graze relatively free from human interference. Standing about six feet tall and armed with long, curving horns the yak is able to defend itself against any natural predator. When danger threatens the adults form themselves into a solid mass around the young. A similar technique is employed by the smaller musk ox (*Ovibos moschatus*) (left and bottom right) which lives on the open tundra of northern Canada and Greenland. Musk ox live together in herds which range from half a dozen to almost a hundred in strength and survive the winter blizzards by huddling together for warmth. Faced by danger, the American bison (*Bison bison*) (below, below left and bottom left) may stand docile or run in panic-stricken stampede.

The open grasslands of Africa are home to immense numbers of antelopes and gazelles, all of which belong to the Bovid family, a more familiar member of which is the domestic cow. Below and facing page top: The springbok (*Antidorcas marsupialis*) which is found in large numbers in South Africa, and is that nation's national animal. When alarmed the springbok will flee and then suddenly leap over 10 feet into the air, perhaps in an attempt to shake of pursuing predators. Bottom left: A male greater kudu (*Strepsiceros strepsiceros*) showing the impressive horns which made this creature a favourite target of big game hunters. Bottom right: The elegant steinbuck (*Raphicerus campestris*), one of the smallest of the antelopes. Right: A pair of young impala (*Aepyceros melampus*) at dawn. Facing page bottom: A female nyala (*Tragelaphus angasi*) a rare forest antelope which has only recently been bred in captivity with any success.

Top left: A defassa waterbuck (*Kobus defassa*) displaying its impressive horns. Right: A female defassa waterbuck with its young. Facing page top: A herd of defassa waterbuck in lush riverside vegetation. Above: One of the elegant gemsbok (*Oryx gazella*) which inhabit the deserts of southwestern Africa, together with smaller gazelles. This fleet-footed creature is ideally suited to its arid environment and can go long periods without water, gaining its moisture from the plants it eats. Centre right: The topi, a sub-species of the Haartebeest (*Alcelaphus buselaphus*). Top right: A vast herd of wildebeest (*Connochaetes taurinus*) moves across the Serengeti grasslands in East Africa. These creatures undertake seasonal migrations as the dry season approaches and pastures far from water dry out. At such times they may gather together in herds numbering many thousands.

These pages: The impala (*Aepyceros melampus*) is one of the most graceful creatures in Africa. It ranges widely across sub-Saharan Africa, preferring open woodland and the fringes of grassy plains. This nimble creature has learnt to be very wary and seeks shelter in bush and forest whenever danger threatens, being able to cover distances of around 30 feet in a single bound. It is therefore rarely found far from cover, and never ventures on to open country.

Top: The wild Asian buffalo (*Bubalus arnee*), otherwise known as the water buffalo, lives in swamps and marshes in India and Southeast Asia. Wild populations have declined seriously, but it has been domesticated and is kept in large numbers. Above and facing page top: The African buffalo (*Synceros caffer*) has never been domesticated as it is an aggressive creature which will charge if disturbed. Facing page bottom: A white faced gnu (*Connochaetus taurinus*).

Like the elephants, the rhinoceros family was much more numerous a few million years ago than it is today. It included graceful running animals and the largest land mammal ever to live as well as creatures very like modern rhinoceroses. Today only a handful of species survive, and several of these are in danger of extinction. The two most numerous species are those from Africa. Facing page bottom: The white rhinoceros (*Ceratotherium simum*) is the largest of all and lives on open country in South and East Africa. It grazes on the savannah and is frequently seen in small herds, rarely objecting to human presence. Far more aggressive is the black rhinoceros (*Diceros bicornis*) (remaining pictures) which can measure 12 feet in length and lives on the East African plains. Largely a nocturnal browser, the black rhinoceros will launch a ferocious charge, quite capable of overturning a truck, if it is disturbed.

These pages: The hippopotamus (*Hippopotamus amphibius*), of which there are two distinct species, is a characteristic animal of Africa and is restricted to that continent. Early European explorers of Africa who found hippopotami in the River Niger in West Africa thought that they had found a tributary of the Nile, for it was thought that this was the only river in which the creatures were found. It is now known that hippotami inhabit lakes and rivers throughout Africa. They spend most of the day wallowing in the water, emerging at night to graze and browse on waterside vegetation. In many areas the lack of any tall riverside plants is a good indication of large numbers of hippopotami. The creatures live together in herds, and can be a considerable hazard to navigation of the rivers. Left: The young are born in the rainy season, at which time the adults become aggressive.

The savannah of East Africa is famous for the vast herds of hoofed mammals which roam the open spaces in their thousands. Of these the most striking is surely the zebra with its bold black and white markings. These stripes are actually a form of camouflage for they serve to break up the outline of the zebra and confuse the lions which prey on them. The common zebra (*Equus burchelli*) shown here is by far the most numerous. The larger Grevy's zebra (*Equus grevyi*) is restricted to northeastern Africa, but is still present in large numbers. Only a few hundred of the mountain zebra (*Equus zebra*) survive in reserves while the quagga (*Equus quagga*) became extinct in 1883.

These pages: To many scientists the giraffe (*Giraffa camelopardalis*) is a beast living in the wrong era. Ten million years ago numerous highly specialised species of mammal were alive, but they have all vanished to be replaced by more adaptable types as the climate has changed. But the giraffe, fitted to a life in open woodland has survived. Even so its numerous relatives in Asia and Europe have long since died out. The biggest giraffes can reach 20 feet in height and so can pluck leaves from the highest branches. The long legs enable the giraffe to out-run predators, and if cornered can be used as effective flailing weapons to drive attackers away. However the long neck and gangly legs have their disadvantages, one of which is revealed when drinking. In order the bring the head down to water level the giraffe must spread its legs wide and crouch down low. In such a position the giraffe is vulnerable to attack and must remain alert.

Bottom left: A playful pair of African ground squirrels (*Xerus erythropus*). These sociable creatures live together in communal burrows and always greet each other with a brief tail-waving display. They readily take to life in city suburbs, feeding on seeds and fruits. Mongooses are famous for their ability to prey on venomous snakes which would normally prey on mammals the size of mongooses. They also attack rodents and, indeed, any animal of a suitable size. This hunting skill and its easily tamed nature has made the mongoose a favoured household pet throughout much of its range and has led to its introduction on islands, such as Hawaii, where rats were infesting crops and towns. Facing page, left and bottom right: The yellow mongoose. Below left: The dwarf mongoose (*Helogale undulata rufula*). Below: The banded mongoose (*Mungos mungo*) which inhabits the African savannah, preying on lizards, birds and insects as well as snakes and rodents.

Top: The American beaver (*Castor canadensis*) which live together in small family groups. Beavers are famous for their building skills, using hundreds of saplings and trees to build into dams and lodges. The dams are plastered with mud to make them waterproof and block streams to form large ponds. In the pond the beavers build the lodge, or home, with its protected underwater entrance.
Above: A fox squirrel (*Sciurus niger*) which is common in the forests of the Appalachians and other deciduous forests of the United States. Above right: A long-tailed weasel (*Mustela frenata*) rears up to scan the land for prey in Montana. Above right: A ground squirrel (*Citllus armatus*) in Yellowstone.
Right: A hoary marmot (*Marmota callgata*) found in the mountains of North America.
Facing page: A blacktail Prairie Dog (*Cynomys ludovicianus*).

Top left: The American red squirrel (*Tamiasciurus hudsonicus*) which feeds on berries, nuts and bark during the winter months. Top right: The European red squirrel (*Sciurus vulgaris*) has been largely replaced in Britain by the American grey squirrel (*Sciurus carolinensis*) (above centre). Large numbers still thrive on the continent, however, and sometimes undertake migrations over hundreds of miles in groups of several thousand individuals. Above: The European hedgehog (*Erinaceus europaeus*) which comes out at night to search for earthworms and other invertebrates. When threatened the hedgehog rolls itself up and erects its spines to form a nearly invulnerable coat. There is evidence that hedgehogs are learning to vary this behaviour when startled by strong light. Instead of rolling up they scamper off, and so avoiding being run over by motor vehicles. Left: A young brown hare (*Lepus europaeus*). Facing page: A fox squirrel (*Sciurus niger*).

Top left: The European mink (*Lutreola lutreola*) began to decline in numbers around 1880 due to the loss of its secluded riverbank habitat and is now extinct in much of the continent. The high value of the animal's fur has led to its being kept on farms by humans together with the American mink (*Lutreola vison*) (facing page) and several colour variations have arisen. Top left: An African hedgehog (*Erinaceus albiventris*) curled up in its defensive ball. Above: A juvenile European badger (*Meles meles*), a heavy bodied creature which preys on invertebrates and small mammals as well as scavenging. Above right: A European otter (*Lutra lutra*), a creature threatened with extinction. Right: The common palm civet (*Paradoxurus hermaphroditus*) from India and Sri Lanka. Far right: A stoat (*Mustela ermina*) emerges from a rabbit warren after an unsuccessful hunt.

The rodents are the most successful of all mammals existing in vast numbers and including more species than any other group. About one third of all mammal species are rodents and an even higher proportion of absolute numbers. Top left: The brown rat (*Rattus norvegicus*) is a typically urban species living in sewers and cellars and breeding at a prolific rate. Top right: The deer mouse (*Peromyscus maniculatus*) of North America which feeds on invertebrates and plants. Above: The salt marsh harvest mouse (*Eithrodentomys raviventris*) building its summer nest prior to giving birth to a litter of four. Above right and facing page top: the house mouse (*Mus musculus*), a pest which has followed man around the world. Right: A harvest mouse (*Micromys minutus*) which is adept at climbing grass stems in search of food. Facing page bottom: A water vole (*Arvicola terrestris*) which lives along European river banks.

Top left: The Canadian porcupine (*Erethizon dorsatum*) is found not only in Canada, but also throughout much of the United States. Right: The tree porcupine (*Coendou prehensilis*) of Guyana is typical of South American porcupines in having a prehensile tail which is an aid in climbing. Top right and facing page: The raccoon which is native to the forests of North America, but has recently moved into urban areas as a nocturnal scavenger. Above centre: A beautifully marked lesser panda (*Ailurus fulgens*) of the Himalayas which is the only living relative of the better-known giant panda and shares its liking for bamboo, though it will take fruit and small animals as well. Above: The capybara (*Hydrochoerus hydrocaeris*) of the South America is the largest rodent in the world, tipping the scales at 130 pounds.

The closely related lynx (*Felis lynx*) (bottom) and bobcat (*Felis rufus*) (remaining pictures) were until recently classed together in the same genus *Lynx*, but are now classed together with most other cats as *Felis*. The lynx is a widespread cat which ranges across Europe, northern Asia and the northern part of North America. It is heavily dependent on hares and rodents for its diet. The cyclic rising and falling of hare populations over a period of some years has a dramatic effect on lynx populations. The slightly smaller bobcat lives throughout North America, south of the range of the lynx, preying on similar victims, together with a large proportion of birds. Both species are largely nocturnal so it is extremely difficult to be certain as to population levels and some authorities claim that they should be classed as endangered.

Bottom right: A jaguarundi (*Panthera jaguarundi*) pauses in its hunt to study the photographer in the Sonoran Desert. This elegant cat ranges widely between Texas and the River Plate, preying on a variety of small animals. Its body structure is similar to the earliest cat ancestors of around 35 million years ago. Remaining pictures: The cougar (*Felis concolor*), also known as the puma or mountain lion, is the largest cat in North America. It can grow up to 8 feet in length and is capable of bringing down prey as large as deer and young cattle. Until the coming of European civilisation the cougar was found throughout the entire Americas, but has now been pushed out of much of its range by extensive agriculture and by stockmen all too aware of the cougar's taste for domestic animals. In the more remote regions, however, this powerful cat continues to thrive, hunting at night and dusk and lying up during the daylight hours.

Top left: The caracal (*Felis caracal*) is an unusual cat with its long, dog-like legs and long pointed ears. It is about three feet in length and preys upon a wide range of smaller animals, including rodents, reptiles and birds. The caracal's skill at hunting birds has made it unpopular with farmers throughout its range from South Africa to Bangladesh for it is equally adept at taking domestic fowls. Remaining pictures: The serval cat (*Felis serval*) has a similar skill at taking poultry, but tends to concentrate more on medium-sized mammals and on wild birds, which it climbs trees to seize in their night-time roosts. The serval is restricted to sub-Saharan Africa and is easily recognised by its boldly marked coat. Infrequent reports of a black serval have been made from upland Kenya, but the degree of affinity between the two types of animal is unclear.